M

PLANT CLOSINGS
Worker Rights, Management Rights and the Law

SP PC SOCIAL
PHILOSOPHY
& POLICY CENTER

PLANT CLOSINGS
Worker Rights, Management Rights and the Law

Francis A. O'Connell, Jr.

Transaction Books
New Brunswick (USA) and London (UK)

Published by the Social Philosophy and Policy Center
and by Transaction, Inc. 1986

Library of Congress Cataloging-in-Publication Data

O'Connell, Francis A., Jr., 1914-
  Plant closings.

  (Studies in social philosophy & policy; no. 7)
  Includes bibliographical references.
  1. Plant shutdowns — Law and legislation — United
States — Cases. 2. Plant shutdowns — Law and legislation —
United States. I. Title. II. Series.
KF3471.A7025 1986   344.7301259   85-63439
ISBN 0-912051-07-8   347.3041259
ISBN 0-912051-08-6 (pbk.)

Cover Design: Jacky Ahrens

To Lonnie, whose patient understanding and
fierce protectionism made it possible

ACKNOWLEDGEMENTS

The use of "we" throughout the text is neither regal nor modest, nor is it merely editorial. This book has been, save for its very last stages, a collaborative effort. The original idea was Professor Richard McKenzie's, and to the extent that the finished product contains any comprehensible economics, they are his. To the extent that it has a properly scholarly tone, that, too, is largely due to his benign influence. To the extent that it falls short in either of those respects, the responsibility is mine.

So, also, in respect of any other imperfections which may have crept in, notwithstanding the devoted and invaluable assistance of three crack labor law scholars—my friend Edward B. Miller, former Chairman of the National Labor Relations Board (NLRB), my stepson William F. Grant of the NLRB, and Professor Leonard Bierman of Texas A & M University. Credit (and no blame) belongs also to numerous other friends and former colleagues—Peter Nash, Jay Siegal, and John Jay stand out —whom I called upon, from time to time, for information or assistance, and who responded without fail and always helpfully.

Still, this work would not have seen the light of day without Ellen Frankel Paul of the Social Philosophy and Policy Center at Bowling Green State University, a woman with the patience of a saint and the enthusiasm of a teenager. And it would have emerged looking rather shabby indeed were it not for the lynx-eyed copyediting of the meticulous Joan Kennedy Taylor.

Finally, a special garland to Joanna Smiley of Aptos, California— more than a secretary, more than a mediatrix between me and the sophisticated incompetence of the computerized word processor—a patient, diligent, and devoted friend.

To all of them I give my deepest gratitude and add the hopeless wish that I have repaid them by writing a better book.

Frank O'Connell
Aptos, California
January 1986

TABLE OF CONTENTS

PREFACE

We live in an age of rights. More accurately, perhaps, ours is an era characterized by an intense *preoccupation* with "rights" of one kind or another. We seem to be asserting rights, defining them, debating them—incessantly.* Some of those rights are traditional, in the sense that they spring from natural or constitutional law, statutory enactment, or the common law of contracts or torts. That is to say, they either inhere in or have been conferred upon the person or they derive from the ownership of property and entail the exercise of dominion over it. They are conferred by the legislature (or, as happens with increasing frequency these days, by the judiciary acting legislatively), or they arise out of contracts or other voluntary transactions. Examples come readily to mind: land-use rights (law), the right to unemployment insurance (legislature) and to an integrated education (judiciary), or the right to occupy a dwelling under a lease (contract). Standing atop them all, of course, are the natural, "unalienable" rights with which men are "endowed by their Creator" and the constitutional rights which they enjoy as members of a free society. All true rights in our society must stem from one or another of these sources.

Lately, however, we have seen the rise of what might be called pseudo-rights. Their roots are not to be found in laws or contracts. Indeed, they often are not rights in any real legal sense at all, but simply *desiderata* of one sort or another—often running counter to traditional legal principles. They are called "rights" for a very good reason: our society is generally and traditionally hospitable to rights and hostile to their suppression or infringement. Hence, to attach the nomenclature of rights to what, at bottom, may be little more than unsupported demands or aspirations has been found useful by partisans. Frequently, it makes possible the achievement of some goal which has proved difficult or impossible to achieve through traditional channels. Labeling the goal a right makes an enormous—often crucial—difference.

If the foregoing strikes some as excessively elementary, the excuse is that these reflections on the nature of rights seemed a necessary background against which to examine the various rights with which this study is concerned. In one way or another and to one degree or another,

---

*See *Disabling America: The "Rights Industry" in Our Time* by Professor Richard E. Morgan, Chairman of the Department of Government at Bowdoin College (New York: Basic Books, 1984). An extreme example of the epidemic of "rights" terminology—of the tendency to confuse a claim on compassion with a right—was recently observed in California. A bumper sticker spunkily asserted: "Animals Have Rights Too." It appeared on a pickup truck with California plates, but, lest too much be read into that, it should be added that the bumper sticker proclaimed its source as The Fund for Animals in New York City.

PREFACE

the rights asserted by or on behalf of various actors in a plant-closing drama exhibit just about all of the characteristics we have just described, both for "rights" and for "pseudo-rights." If we are to sort them out and judge their merits, we must do so using the traditional criteria by which asserted rights are tested and conflicts of law are resolved.

What, precisely, is the content of "the worker's right to his job," to take one phrase which has been appearing with greater and greater frequency? In what respects is the right founded on traditional rights theory and in what respects might it be said to be merely a pseudo-right? Is it a sort of prescriptive right, acquired over time simply by working for a given employer? Is it something less—a right to notice, severance pay, and, perhaps, other benefits on termination, as prescribed in so-called plant-closing legislation? Is there a right in the job conferred by the National Labor Relations Act (other than those claims and entitlements which may result from collective bargaining under that law)?

Advocates of each of these views exist. Their rationale needs to be analyzed. A sorting out of substance and terminology is an indispensable prerequisite to any attempt to assess the validity of the claim of either workers' rights or management rights in plant-closing situations and to any attempt to resolve analytically the conflict between the two. Clarifying the terms of the public debate on so important a subject would seem, in itself, to be a worthy objective for this study.

But it has even more ambitious objectives: By defining and delimiting the terms "workers' rights" and "management rights," and proposing accommodations where they conflict, this study hopes to narrow the area of genuine conflict and thereby contribute to its peaceful and appropriate resolution. Among other things, it hopes to demonstrate to the advocates of so-called plant-closing legislation that a good deal of what they seek to accomplish is already in place or achievable under existing law—both contract and tort law, as well as the National Labor Relations Act (NLRA).

This study aims also at the policy makers. As in the case of any other right or privilege, there are strong arguments to be made against doctrinaire and unrestrained assertion or enforcement of rights, however genuine and well founded they may be. (Needless to say, the argument is even more powerful in the case of rights of dubious provenance.) "Your right to swing your arm stops where my nose begins" is not just a colorful aphorism. It is a fundamental principle of a society of free and responsible individuals. It is another way of saying that every right gives rise to a duty—sometimes negative (keep off my grass), sometimes positive. In the latter case, someone (employers, taxpayers) has a duty to respond to the claimant's claim.

PREFACE

Obviously, then, a right in respect of a job (whatever it may consist of) implies some invasion or diminution of the right of the owner of the enterprise which provides the job, i.e., the employer. It may be accomplished by mutual agreement (the preferred mode in our transactional society) or it may be imposed by law. If the latter, what justification can be offered for it? And how far may it extend before it becomes manifestly improper, both as an invasion of property rights and as a matter of legal and socio-economic policy?

More specifically, how widely can the concept and costs of "workers' rights" be applied in plant-closing situations before they can be said to interfere unduly with (a) management's inherent right to run the enterprise, and (b) the efficacy and mobility of capital in a free market economy? Conversely, how absolute are management rights? How much interference with them can be argued to be a proper and essential ingredient of a humane economy? These questions have never been more timely, given the incessant assault on property rights which has come to characterize our polity. Policy makers have never been more in need of enlightenment and guidance. Happily, this study offers both!

We begin with an overview of the origin of the problem and the nature of the issues with which our study deals. This is followed by a brief examination of so-called plant-closing legislation. What rights does such legislation aim at conferring? On whom? At whose expense? What are the arguments for and against it? We then proceed to an area which has been generally overlooked in the workers' rights debate: the National Labor Relations Act. The object is to examine the way in which a law already on the books—the Act recently celebrated its fiftieth anniversary—has been or can be utilized to accomplish (for unionized workers, at least) much of what is sought by plant-closing laws. This involves an extensive analysis of decisions of the National Labor Relations Board (NLRB) and the courts, chiefly in the area of the duty imposed by the Act on employers to bargain with the unions of their employees concerning managerial decisions which will eliminate jobs. Again, as in the case of plant-closing legislation, this study evaluates what is aimed at in the way of workers' rights, what has been achieved, and with what impact on the employers involved, on the rest of the economy, and on the law.

We then turn to an analysis of "job rights" as a legal and economic concept, and we explore sources of workers' rights to be found in traditional contract and tort law.

We conclude with some modest proposals to employers and unions for the accommodative resolution of the tensions between workers' rights and management rights.

PREFACE

A personal postscript: The author spent forty years in the field of labor law and employee relations. Except for a brief stretch of government service, all of those years were spent on the management side of the table. It would be fatuous to assert or assume that the present writing is not influenced by that experience—that it does not reflect, as Justice Cardozo put it, "the likes and dislikes, the predilections and the prejudices, the complex of instincts and emotions and habits and convictions, which make the man."* We are each the product of our own cumulative experience, and we carry it to each new task we address.

I have tried, nevertheless, to be objective, fair, *professional.* Absolute evenhandedness is probably beyond my grasp, after all those years on one side, and it would produce, in any case, a study at once stupifyingly bland and flagrantly disobedient of my editor's stern injunction to "express a point of view."

With these confessions I hope to disarm and engage readers whose experience and sympathies may lie on the other side of the playing field.

Francis A. O'Connell, Jr.
Aptos, California
December 1985

---

*Cardozo, *The Nature of the Judicial Process* (New Haven: Yale University Press, 1971), p. 167.

I. The Problem, The Issues, and The Scope of The Study

"Creative destruction" was the phrase that Joseph Schumpeter, the late, great Harvard economist, coined to describe the process by which a capitalist economy sustains and continuously renews itself. The process involves innovation, improvement, modification—and, now and then, failure and abandonment. Sometimes the process is activated by obsolescence, sometimes by technology, and sometimes by costs of production or marketing which come to be deemed intolerable. Depending on the nature of the activating circumstances, companies have folded, changed direction, or relocated operations to areas closer to markets or to areas where labor costs were less or where other advantages were present or disadvantages absent.

The process is not without pain and casualties. Companies—whole industries—have disappeared. The people who depended on them for a living were faced, often with little advance notice, or sometimes none at all, with the fact that their jobs had disappeared—in all likelihood permanently. Sometimes other jobs were available, but increasingly the displaced employees found themselves in a locality where high unemployment was endemic and permanent. Some looked for and found employment in other regions.¹ Others did not. Some never did. The transition from employed to unemployed, producer to pauper, traumatized some permanently. Ghost towns in the West, the abandoned textile and shoe towns of the Northeast, and the "pockets of poverty" in Appalachia testify to the fact that some places and some people never recovered.

Throughout industrial history until relatively recent times, such dislocations and tragedies were treated more or less as though they were natural disasters. The right of the owner of a business to shut it down or move it or otherwise obey economic imperatives was unabridged. The consequences for employees of the enterprise were considered unfortunate but inevitable. People were thrown on their own resources just as if the plant had been swept away by a hurricane or a flood. Some made it. Some did not, but, in any event, that was not in times past considered to be a case for intervention by government. Still less was it deemed a duty of the beleaguered enterprise to deploy its resources in cushioning the impact on employees.

Beginning with the Great Depression of the 1930s, however, the pattern has changed. Government intervention in all kinds of social and economic situations became acceptable, and governments soon began shifting some of the burden of economic dislocation to business. (Unemployment insurance is an example.) Whether a cause or an effect of this massive change in our prevailing notions of political philosophy and economy, public attitudes toward those suffering economic adversity changed. Society had always acknowledged a duty toward its less fortunate members—toward those unable to help themselves—but now compassion was expanded to reach those disadvantaged by economic forces beyond their control. This marked a quantum change from the prevailing ethos during the Great Depression when, as has frequently been remarked, the unemployed felt a great sense of personal guilt from the mere fact of their unemployment, however blameless they were.[2] The "Politics of Compassion" became the accepted order—a signal, perhaps, that a new stage of "advanced capitalism" had been reached. In any case, the economic phenomenon described generically as "plant closing" (as used in this study, the term embraces everything from a going-out-of-business shutdown to a geographic relocation of operations, unless some further specificity is required) began to attract attention. Widely publicized industrial movements from the so-called Snow Belt to the Sun Belt undoubtedly were a contributing factor, as was the recession of the early eighties. Some of the attention paid to the phenomenon was purely economic. Some of it was clearly political, and, in some cases, the therapy of choice was fundamental change in our institutional structure and our political arrangements. But all of it was stimulated by the problems created by plant closings. Management decisions to close or relocate plants, and the implementation of such decisions, began to come under scrutiny and attack as being exclusively oriented toward costs and profits, and exhibiting little or no concern for costs in human terms. The result has been a plea for government intervention to regulate plant closures and to require compensation payments to those affected by them. Not surprisingly, the debate centers on rights—the relatively new concept of "workers' rights in their jobs" versus the traditional right of the owner of a business to manage it and to deploy his assets as the economic circumstances require.

The management side of this rights debate has trouble matching the revolutionary appeal of a slogan like "workers' rights." Its arguments, though solid, are simply not as exciting.[3] They rest on property rights and the imperatives of a market economy. The right of managers to manage—free of any need to consult with unions over managerial decisions or to buy off "job rights"—is unquestionable in a property-based economy, they argue, and ought not to be clouded or encumbered, at least not any more than it already is. The proper discharge of the responsibility of managers to manage capital assets prudently, the argument runs, is in the interest not just of the owners of those assets, but also of the economy at large and, therefore, of the larger society. That responsibility is not borne by, and cannot be shared with, employees and their unions, for it is irresponsible to demand the involvement of persons in decisions when they have no responsibility for their outcome. Moreover, opponents argue, to delay essential management decision making or its implementation by requiring that employees and their unions be given an opportunity to participate, and to add still other and more explicit costs to essential management reaction to economic conditions, is to place a heavy burden on the enterprise and to cripple that mobility of both capital and labor which is an indispensable element of a free market economy. Marginal plants will be driven under and new plants and new jobs will never come into existence. Thus the sides lined up several years ago.

But the debate is not just between the advocates of workers' rights (whatever our analysis may show them to consist of) on the one hand and the defenders of property rights or management rights on the other, although surely that is the most visible aspect of the debate. The case for workers' rights is more complex, and the arguments against the concept as it has been advanced are more subtle than labels or slogans make it seem.

Can there be an inherent right in or to a job which is derived simply from working at that job over a period of time? Can the legislature constitutionally create workers' rights by inhibiting the traditional right of the owner to shut down his plant or to move it? Is the National Labor Relations Board authorized to create such a right out of the collective bargaining provisions of the National Labor Relations Act?

If the answer to any or all of these questions is "yes," does the law thereby create an impediment to the mobility of capital which is inconsistent with a free market economy and, on that account, ultimately injurious to the interest of the workers in whose behalf the inhibitions upon plant closure are invoked in the first place? Probably. But the dislocated workers and their unions understandably take the shorter-range view of their interests. When Jerry J. Jasinowski of the National

Association of Manufacturers asks[4] "Does it make sense to jeopardize competitiveness and the employees of a California plant because an Illinois plant is no longer viable?" the answer he gets back from Illinois is loudly affirmative. To those employees it makes all kinds of sense!

The contest between the conflicting views is currently being played out in all three arenas of our government: legislative, executive, and judicial. The legislative approach involves attempts, at both federal and state levels, to enact laws to regulate and to impose costs upon plant closings; the executive aspect chiefly involves administrative interpretations and decisions of the National Labor Relations Board under the National Labor Relations Act;[5] and the judicial role involves (a) the review by the federal appellate courts (especially the Supreme Court of the United States) of the decisions of the NLRB under the Act, and (b) more recently, lawsuits for damages brought by employees displaced by plant closings. This study examines all three areas, commencing with the legislative (the drive for so-called plant-closing laws).

II. The Legislative Approach

Since 1979 there have been upwards of two dozen plant-closing bills introduced in the legislatures of various states, as well as in the United States Congress.

The state legislative proposals have a common thrust: the imposition of costs on plant closings—short, however, of attempting otherwise to prevent or prohibit such closings.[1] As described by Professor Finis Welch, a prominent labor economist at the University of California, Los Angeles, who studied them all in 1984, "provisions of proposed legislation encompass requirements for specific periods of notification to employees (up to two years in some cases), severance pay—which would be determined by length of service and past earnings—and continuation of health insurance benefits. Restitution to affected communities has been proposed, as have government subsidies to worker or community groups for purchase of defunct plants or companies."[2] Professor Welch finds all such legislation counterproductive, not only for the business involved and other businesses which might otherwise arise following a plant closure, but also for the employees involved and other workers who will not be employed in new enterprises.

Although legislation is very much a part of the workers' rights debate these days, it is interesting that none of the state bills undertakes to create or confer a right *in* or *to* a job, such as would require employers to "buy out" such rights, and would permit employees (by refusing to "sell") to delay, block, or compel the revocation of a decision to close a plant. The extent of the right created by state plant-closing proposals, therefore, is not much more than simply an entitlement to notice and compensation when jobs are extinguished. There is no employee right to *prevent* the extinguishment.

The same thing cannot be said, as we shall see, of the rights which employees enjoy under the National Labor Relations Act. Although recent interpretations of the Act fall short of explicitly creating a right *in* the job, they go a long way in that direction by entitling unions and their members in certain circumstances to participate (via the mandatory

bargaining process) in the managerial decision-making process preceding
an actual plant closure, and, in the course of such participation, to delay
and possibly bring about the modification or revocation of the plant-
closing decision. This is considerably closer (in the situations in which the
bargaining duty applies) to a substantive "right in the job"—although
still falling short of a genuine property right—than is provided under any
plant-closing statute yet proposed, save one.

The exception is the "Labor-Management Notification and Consultation Act of 1985." It was introduced by Representative William D. Ford,
a Michigan Democrat with strong ties to organized labor. Although the
bill was subsequently voted down by the House of Representatives
(208-203), it is worth a brief analysis, partly because it illustrates one
dimension of the struggle over plant-closing policy and partly because,
for reasons which will appear, it is unlikely that Congress has heard the
last of Representative Ford's efforts.

Interestingly enough, Congressman Ford's 1985 bill was considerably
—almost totally—different from his earlier passes at the plant-closing
problem, which resembled, rather closely, the state legislative efforts
already described.³ Mr. Ford's 1985 bill seemed deliberately to trespass
on the territory of the National Labor Relations Board. There is, we
think, a rather interesting political reason for this, but it is better discussed after a brief examination of what Representative Ford's bill
sought to do.

First of all, what it did *not* do is to require the payment of severance
pay, as the state proposals do. It did *more*—or, at least, it set up the
potential for *unionized* employees to achieve more than that—through a
compulsory bargaining process of its own, which was quite clearly in
direct competition with the National Labor Relations Act. To that extent
(like the NLRA itself, as was just observed), it came a good deal closer
than state plant-closing legislation does to creating a right in the job.
This it did by way of a right to negotiate over the plant-closing decision.

Descriptions of the purposes of legislation, as contained in the legislation itself, are rarely models of candor and full disclosure, and Mr.
Ford's bill was no exception. It stated its purpose as follows: "To require
employers to notify and consult with employees before ordering a plant
closing or permanent layoff."

Actually, it did a great deal more.⁴ For one thing, "plant closing" and
"permanent layoff" (at least in the usual sense of those terms) do not by
any means define the limits of the reach of Mr. Ford's bill. Extra territory was embraced by a series of definitions which enormously expanded the terms used. Thus, "permanent layoff" was defined as

including an "employment loss" which, in turn, is defined as including a "reduction in hours of work of more than 50 percent during any six month period." Obviously, then, a temporary layoff of ninety days (half of a six-month period) could result in a 50 percent reduction of hours for the affected employees, and thus a temporary layoff was transformed into a permanent layoff under the bill, vastly expanding the bill's intrusion into the managerial decision-making area. Considering that employees affected by such short-term layoffs are almost invariably covered by unemployment insurance of one kind or another, it is obvious that the ill which Congressman Ford was aiming at was *dislocation,* not loss of wages.

Another example (still bearing in mind the legislative sleight of hand just described): the bill as introduced would have been triggered by an "employment loss" (as already defined) for fifty or more employees at a given plant site. Thus a layoff of as few as fifty employees could trigger the provisions of the bill even though they were a quantitatively insignificant part of a plant employing many thousands of employees, the remainder of whom were not to be affected by the shutdown decision.

The Ford bill prohibited a covered employer (and anyone with fifty or more employees could be covered) from ordering a plant closing or a permanent layoff without giving notice to the union representing the affected employees or to the employees themselves.[5] The bill went on to require that, in addition to notification, the employer had a duty of "meeting" and "consulting in good faith" with the union representative.

A couple of observations are appropriate at this point. First, the language was almost identical with that of the National Labor Relations Act with respect to the latter's description of collective bargaining.[6] The Ford bill, however, went somewhat further. It stated that the "consultation" (i.e., bargaining) is "for the purpose of agreeing to a modification or alternative" to the shutdown or layoff decision.[7] No provision was made for even the *possibility*—however remote—that the management decision would remain unaffected! Thus Congressman Ford went a good deal further than the National Labor Relations Act, which confines itself to requiring the employer to meet and confer in good faith "with respect to wages, hours," etc. The outcome is not dictated or assumed, as in the Ford bill. Indeed, the National Labor Relations Act has provided since 1947 that the duty to bargain does *not* "compel either party to agree to a proposal or require the making of a concession."

A few more provocative highlights and we shall leave the Ford bill. The Federal Mediation and Conciliation Service—a *mediating* agency—

was given something of an *adversarial* role. It was to be the judge of whether an employer, by failing to provide "relevant" information necessary to a "thorough evaluation" of the proposed plant closing or permanent layoff, had been guilty of a failure to consult in good faith. And what if the Mediation Service decided that the employer had been guilty of such failure? Congressman Ford's bill was curiously silent on this point. A fair reading of it, however, suggested that the next thing would be a report to the Secretary of Labor, who was given the duty of investigating any complaint alleging that an employer has ordered a plant closing or permanent layoff in violation of the bill. Again, the bill was silent as to the possible sources of such a complaint. But again, an educated guess is possible: two prime candidates to blow the whistle were (1) the union and (2) the Mediation Service.

In any case, the Secretary of Labor would have had powers under the Ford bill which are analogous to those of the National Labor Relations Board—so much so that, if the two were unions, one could anticipate a violent jurisdictional dispute. For example, if the Secretary decided that a complaint against an employer was well founded, he was *required* to seek an injunction and, among other things, the court could be asked to order the reinstatement of any employees terminated or laid off from the closed plant or operation. The employer was also made subject to a civil action for damages on behalf of any employee who suffered an "employment loss."[8] The suit could be brought by an individual or his union, and could also be brought on behalf of others similarly situated. Clearly, it was Representative Ford's intention to persuade employers that the costs of a shutdown can be heavy indeed—maybe intolerable—and therefore not to be risked.

As we noted earlier, the Ford bill failed to get by the House, despite the Democratic majority. We have nevertheless devoted time to this analysis because the narrowness of the vote (208-203) indicates that Mr. Ford is not alone in his concern for the problem, nor in his approach to it, although obviously his colleagues do not share all his instincts and motivations.

Moreover, there is an aspect of the Ford bill which interestingly illuminates another aspect of the plant-closing debate. It can be stated this way: Why did so devoted a friend of organized labor as Congressman Ford push a bill so clearly calculated to duplicate the functions in plant-closing cases of the National Labor Relations Board, historically seen as the union's instrumentality, rather than the employer's? The answer lies in the well-publicized hostility of organized labor to the philosophy and policies in labor matters of Ronald Reagan's administration, including

Mr. Reagan's appointees to the Board. Inasmuch as the "Reagan Board" is hereafter discussed in some detail in Chapter VII, it will suffice here simply to mention that its decisions have so offended organized labor that the AFL-CIO has variously threatened to boycott the Board or to seek repeal of the National Labor Relations Act. In any case, it is clear that unions do not feel that the Board's processes will, during this administration, be effectively employed in their behalf, in plant-closing situations or any others. Hence the unusual alternative of setting up a rival agency was pursued by Congressman Ford, and this may explain why the Ford bill departed so sharply from the approach of earlier plant-closing bills, including his own.

Although the 1985 Ford bill represented a departure from the general pattern of plant-closing legislation, in that it appeared primarily to aim at *deterrence* rather than *compensation,* this is not to suggest that the more typical (compensatory) plant-closing proposal would not also have a deterrent effect. It is not difficult to imagine a shaky company being pushed over the edge by mass desertions of customers, banks, suppliers, and even employees upon making the required announcement of a proposed shutdown. It might seem safer (although not necessarily prudent, if a shutdown is what the circumstances call for) to simply stay put, keep quiet, and muddle through, even though that course may guarantee a shutdown—perhaps bankruptcy—when the hopeless hand has been played.

Similarly, if the law compelled huge cash outlays for severance pay and "restitution" to communities, a marginal company could be fatally weakened. Bleeding slowly but quietly might well be seen as preferable to death by fiscal hemorrhage, and, quite possibly, it would have the advantage of conserving cash for the owners. In many cases, the shutdown of a plant might be occasioned by threatened bankruptcy. The cash penalties required by a plant-closing law could convert that possibility to a certainty. Would this be to the benefit of creditors, employers, or owners—preferable, that is, to trying to work out of the crisis without resorting to bankruptcy? That seems, at best, unlikely. As we have already noted, a strong argument against plant-closing laws is the perverse effect which they would have on capital mobility. We shall return to that subject shortly. Almost equally bad, from the standpoint of the overall economy, is the effect such laws would have on *labor* mobility. Although labor (the individual worker, that is) is not, even today, as mobile as manpower experts sometimes seem to think, still a certain amount of labor mobility is essential—particularly to soak up unemployment. When, to the universal personal disinclination to pull up stakes is added an *incentive* for not doing so—in the form of legislation which operates to keep a plant in place, at least for a time, or which compels the payment of severance pay to the worker-in-place—the negative impact of plant-closing laws on labor mobility (and, therefore, in the end, on the welfare of the very workers the plant-closing law is designed to help) is starkly revealed.

The foregoing summary of some of the principal arguments against plant-closing legislation, brief as it is, serves to point up the fact that, in this area as in so many policy areas, we deal, in a sense, in ethical choices: the interest of the worker (at least short-range) versus the interest of the economy, which is to say, of the public at large. If it were not for the need to strike a balance, it would be easy to let compassion rule, as the advocates of plant-closure regulation argue.[9]

Yet, as we hear over and over again from our political philosophers, government, if and when it intervenes, must do so (and must be seen as doing so) in the "public interest," rather than in the special interest of the few, especially when that interest can only be served at the expense of the many. Is that the case with plant-closure laws? Economists tell us that the larger public interest is served by a healthy, growing economy providing ever more jobs, and that it is disserved by any policy which, by preventing or discouraging "creative destruction," limits capital and labor mobility and retards economic growth, thus, sooner or later, "killing the goose." Government, they argue, if it intervenes at all, ought to be on the side of the goose.

Moreover, the conflict of interests which gives rise to the ethical dilemma just described may be more apparent than real. The same policy which allows capital and labor to move freely to where they can be put to maximum use is a policy which, by the creation of jobs, serves the interest of all workers—even the ones displaced by a plant closing. It is doubtful that the millions of new jobs which our economy has created in just the past few years—an enormously important counterbalance to the widespread layoffs and shutdowns in the so-called smokestack industries—could have been created if capital had not been free to flow where it was needed to start up these new enterprises. Any brake on that mobility would be a direct brake on job creation, including the creation of jobs which may be filled by displaced workers.

Capital which is locked into an unprofitable situation cannot be productive elsewhere. As Professor Richard McKenzie has succinctly observed: "In the end, restrictions on plant closings are restrictions on plant openings."[10]

Thus, the issue of ethics and compassion is narrowed to a consideration of long-range versus short-range interest of workers immediately involved in plant closings. We have already observed that unions and their members tend—perhaps understandably—to take the short-range view. Unions, as institutions, have a further and larger concern. It is, interestingly, one rooted in competition. While unions are, on the one hand, proud of their achievements in collective bargaining, some of them have come to recognize, especially in recent years, that the price of those achievements—higher labor costs to employers—although a plus for them and their members, is a decided negative for their employers when those employers are faced with competition from regions where unions have not gained a hold or have not been so successful in collective bargaining. Employers facing such competition have turned to their unions for some relief from uncompetitive labor costs. A union under pressure for concessions and, at the same time, facing the possibility of mass exodus of employers from its jurisdiction on account of high labor costs, has two options: yield to the demands for concessions, or somehow attempt to halt the exodus. Support of plant-closing laws represents an attempt by unions to adopt the second strategy.[11] It is a strategy of protecting union standards and union members from what might be described as the negative consequences of collective bargaining which has been "too successful."

In any case, there is no doubt that plant-closing laws are effective in delaying or preventing what their proponents call "capital flight." Unfortunately, however, they also have the effect of discouraging industrial movement *into* an area, which is perceived by industry not only as "high cost" in terms of (union negotiated) wages, but also as threatening to impose unacceptable costs on any later need to move out.

Thus, ironically, the plant-closing laws for which unions are pressing (to protect what they have) may, in the event, prove destructive of their interests, as well as of the interests of nonunionized workers in the same area. That such laws may ultimately be more widespread than they are now—at least where unions are strong, politically—is by no means unlikely. Indeed, the improving political prospects for plant-closing legislation[12] have prompted Professor McKenzie to remark, gloomily, that "closing restrictions are a bad idea whose time...may have come."[13]

Plant-closing statutes, however—whether or not they are the wave of the future—are not the only weapon available to unions to battle shutdowns or removals. There is another—the National Labor Relations Act—and we discuss its role and its possibilities in plant removal situations next. First, however, it will be useful to close this chapter by examining one phenomenon of union behavior with respect to plant-closing laws.

That unions should provide such strong support of plant-closing measures is, at first glance, puzzling. It is puzzling because unions, as we shall see, are specially equipped under the National Labor Relations Act to participate on behalf of their members in plant-closing decisions—to create "closing rights" through collective bargaining—and to get the Board to punish plant shutdowns when they are motivated by hostility toward unions. With government intervention thus readily at hand in the form of the compulsory duty of employers to bargain, and with bargaining itself offering endless opportunities for creative solutions tailor-made to the needs of particular groups of workers, why should unions be looking elsewhere?

The answer, understandable upon reflection, is, first, that unions see plant-closing legislation as helpful in those situations in which they may not have the bargaining leverage to get the protections they want in the union contract. The leverage problem is one which unions increasingly face, and it is no coincidence that support for plant-closing laws is particularly strong among those unions (e.g., in the steel and automobile industries) where union bargaining power has been diminished by competitive conditions which occasionally may make plant closure or consolidation a condition of corporate survival. Lacking the power they once had, unions in those industries look to plant-closing laws to prevent or delay cessations of operations and to provide for notice and compensation for their members when the shutdown is no longer avoidable. At the very least (and this is what opponents of plant-closing laws argue most strongly), such legislation, by imposing heavy costs, can delay or forestall implementation of a management decision that a given operation be abandoned or moved to another location with consequent shutdown of the existing plant. Whatever the temporary advantages to the workers-in-place, it is obvious that this sort of impediment to rescue measures is bound to have an adverse effect on companies and employees alike.

Even where union bargaining power has not diminished significantly, unions may prefer to eschew the bargaining process, because (a) they fear (probably rightly) that they might be required to make some undesirable concessions in order to secure the protection in a closing situation that they would wish, and (b) unions have become accustomed in any case to looking toward government to supplement their efforts and to assist in the accomplishment of their bargaining objectives.

Finally, unions are increasingly aware of the *non*union part (upwards of 80 percent) of the private sector work force and, although there is some lag in their recognition of this, they realize that over time their members who are "protected" by state plant-closing constraints may suffer from the competition of workers elsewhere whose employers are not subject to such constraints. It is, therefore, in their perceived interests (shortsighted though this may be) to seek the broadest possible application of plant-closing legislation, which covers union and nonunion plants alike, thus equalizing the disadvantages.

So far we have talked mainly of law. But there is an economic-social cost dimension of which unions are at least subliminally aware. By the enactment of plant-closing laws they are not only relieved from having to trade off something (accept a lower wage, for example) to get rights in the closing situation, but the cost of the measures (including the cost of its ameliorative aspects) are transferred to others by plant-closing laws.

So unions have reasons, satisfactory to themselves, for advocating plant-closing laws even though they have more leverage—and certainly the possibility of achieving something closer to true workers' rights—under the National Labor Relations Act, to which we now turn.

III. Workers' Rights and The National Labor Relations Act

1. Background

For the first century and a half of our existence as a nation, there were no "workers' rights" or "job rights" in the sense in which those terms are being used today. As a contractarian society, all of our employment arrangements not arising out of contract were deemed to be "at will"— that is to say, the arrangement could be terminated by either party at any time.

We are also a property-based society. There was no question, therefore, about the right of the owner of a business to deal with his enterprise (as with his other property) in any lawful manner that suited him. He could change it, sell it, or simply shut it down completely if he chose to do so, and any consideration toward his employees which he might display in any of those circumstances was the product of conscience or compassion, not legal obligation.

These are different times in that respect, as we observed earlier. Yet the basic property-based character of our society has not changed. My son can sell his boat or put it in dry dock or give it away or destroy it. It is his. Scarcely anyone would question his right. I am not free to smash the obnoxiously loud radio of the youngster who lies a few yards from me at the beach. Again, it is his. At the same time, however, I probably can invoke the zoning laws against his father, if the father starts to do something with or to his home or his property which I deem a nuisance and which our codes do not permit.

There have, in short, been abridgements of the concept of unrestricted property rights since John Locke's day, and the National Labor Relations Act[1] represents one of them.

2. The National Labor Relations Act—Overview

At the time of its passage in 1935, one of the chief constitutional complaints against the National Labor Relations Act (aside from the fact that it pushed the Commerce Clause of the Constitution out of shape) was that it massively interfered with freedom of contract. And it did. The employment relationship was pervasively affected. For example, one of the characteristics of at will employment was that an employee could be dismissed for any reason whatever—or none at all. The Act seriously invaded this area. Discharge (or any other kind of discrimination relating to employment) as a reprisal for, or deterrent to, union activity was proscribed as an "unfair labor practice."

Not only were employers no longer to be *absolutely* free to dismiss or discipline their employees, but also, once any union established a majority among their employees, they were compelled to recognize it and deal with it. Gone was the normal freedom of the businessman to decide whom he would or would not do business with. Like it or not, the Act said he would deal with the union chosen by a majority of his employees. Gone also was the freedom to set wages on the basis of the labor market alone. And (a body blow to employment-at-will theory) the Act declared that employees who go on strike remain "employees" within the meaning of the Act. They could not be fired or otherwise punished for striking.

Interference of any kind with the right of employees to join unions was out, including the arrangement (derided by unions as the yellow-dog contract) by which an employee agreed, as a condition of employment, that he would not belong to a union. The introduction of the union as representative precluded (except in special circumstances) any more direct dealing between employer and employee concerning working conditions—another heavy blow to the common-law employment relationship.

Along with these highly significant changes in the contractual aspects of employment came further jolts for property rights, in the form of the Act's basic command that there be no interference of any kind with union organizing. This meant, it transpired, that an employer might even be compelled to allow organizing activities to take place on his plant property.

Although the NLRA (also known as the Wagner Act) was often called a Magna Carta of workers' rights, such rights, as they were then understood, were a far cry from those we are discussing here. No one claimed fifty years ago that the Wagner Act conferred job rights on anybody, save in the sense that an employee now had a right to bargain, through a union, over his wages and other conditions, and he had a right not to be fired (or refused employment) for belonging to that union.

Even today, the Act does not figure prominently in the debate over workers' rights in their jobs. It is not yet widely perceived as a source of

such rights. Yet it should be, for as a result of Board and court interpretations of the Act, it has far more potential than any other legislation
now on the horizon for giving employees an opportunity to challenge a
plant-closing decision and to bring about its modification or even its
reversal. This chapter explores some of those interpretations.

3. Specific Provisions of the Act Relating to Plant Closing

There are two ways in which the Act operates to inject workers and
their unions into the plant-closing situation. One is by way of the
employer's duty to bargain (under section 8(a)(5) of the Act) over wages,
hours, and other terms and conditions of employment. The other is by
way of section 8(a)(3) of the Act which, among other things, brands as an
unfair labor practice the discriminatory termination of employees to
discourage union activity. The two provisions are quite different in purpose and approach.

The duty-to-bargain provisions create an affirmative right on the part
of the employees and their union to participate in the fixing of their
terms of employment. As we shall see, this includes the right to bargain
—at least in some circumstances—in connection with the elimination of
jobs (as by a plant closing), and thus it clearly embodies a workers' right
in respect of the job.

The job-rights aspect of section 8(a)(3), the antidiscrimination provision, is less obvious. The right which it creates is a right to be free of
employer discipline (including discharge) designed to discourage union
activity.

The plant-closing situations with which this study is concerned are
those in which economic reasons dictate the closing. And economics is
the everyday subject matter of collective bargaining. Hence, most of our
attention will be devoted to section 8(a)(5) and the nature and extent of
the employer's duty to bargain in the plant-closing situation. First,
however, we shall dispose of the issue of antiunion motivation in such
situations.

4. Section 8(a)(3) and Plant Closings—Antiunion Animus

The unfair labor practice defined in section 8(a)(3) is aimed at
employer attempts to discourage or punish union activity. It provides, in
part, that it shall be an unfair labor practice for an employer, "(3) By
discrimination in regard to hire or tenure of employment or any term or
condition of employment to encourage or discourage membership in any
labor organization."[2]

Unlike section 8(a)(5) (which calls into play the employer's bargaining duty), section 8(a)(3) does not apply when a plant is shut down solely for economic reasons. It applies only if the shutdown has an antiunion purpose. Economics enters this picture, then, only when it is charged that a plant that was shut down ostensibly for economic reasons was, in fact, closed for the purpose of discouraging unionization. The charge may or may not prove to be well founded, but, in either event, the invocation of section 8(a)(3) puts the shutdown under a cloud and raises the possibility that the Board may act to block the closing or order the closing decision to be reversed, accompanying its order with heavy back pay penalties. This suggests the possible tactical utility of section 8(a)(3) in union organizing situations, and unions, of course, are not unaware of this. An impending or rumored shutdown can be extremely effective as an organizing tool. Workers, previously not organized, may be induced to join a union by the fear of displacement and the union's promise that it will save their jobs. Indeed, unions have been advised by the National Lawyers Guild to make precisely that tactical use of an impending plant closing.[3]

There are other tactical uses of section 8(a)(3) by unions that are worth passing notice. In the 1960s, for example, the author first encountered what became a fairly common technique for unions engaged in organizing campaigns. In conjunction with the demand for recognition as bargaining agent, the union would advise the employer of the names of the members of its in-plant organizing committee. (In former times, it would have kept those names secret for fear of discrimination.) The purpose, of course, was to lay the basis for a charge of discrimination under section 8(a)(3) in the event that any of those individuals was thereafter laid off, demoted, or terminated—whatever the actual reason. The tactic had a tendency to immunize the named individuals from any such employment action, for it could be assumed that it would result in the filing of antiunion discrimination charges against the company.[4]

Moreover, the atmosphere created by such charges would tend to give an antiunion coloration to a subsequent shutdown of the plant. Thus, not only is the initiation of organizational activity shielded by the Act against any employer interference, but even a legitimate (i.e., economically caused) shutdown, occurring thereafter, might have to be defended against charges that it was motivated by hostility toward unionization. Section 8(a)(3), therefore, constitutes both a shield and something a sword for unions in plant-closing situations. As to job rights, it obviously provides something in the way of security for the employee which did not exist before.

But what does all this mean for property rights—the right of the owner to manage his business affairs and dispose of his property? To what extent are those rights abridged and to what extent do they remain untouched by the Act? Like most questions in labor law, there are no simple, unambiguous answers here. Obviously, an employer's property right continues to be absolute, unless and until it conflicts with some right accorded to employees under the Act. As we shall see, there have been great differences of opinion as to just what rights the Act does confer and protect. A few things, however, are clear and can be stated with reasonable certainty. Section 8(a)(3) of the Act does abridge the traditional property rights of the owner in certain circumstances. His right to run the business is modified by the right of his employees to unionize. The owner may not, therefore, in the course of running his business, exercise his managerial rights in a manner calculated to interfere with employee rights under the Act. His right to run the business—to hire and fire—does not include using that right to discourage unionization among his employees. It has also long been accepted that the so-called runaway shop—the removal of operations to another location *for the specific purpose of avoiding or getting rid of a union*—runs afoul of the Act, notwithstanding the traditional right of the owner to move his business about as he chooses.[5] On the other hand, removals or shutdowns for purely economic reasons are not touched by the Act. (As already indicated, however, there are often disputes over how genuine the economic reasons are.)

The Act, in short, does interfere with the rights of the owner of the business when, in the course of running the business, those rights are exercised with what the National Labor Relations Board calls "antiunion animus." But what of the right to go out of business entirely? Is there a right to pack it in, since the idea of dealing with a union is repulsive, something the proprietor simply cannot abide? Is there an absolute right to turn the key and walk away, which (even if exercised out of antiunion animus) the Act does not and cannot touch? Not surprisingly, the NLRB thought not and unions hoped not; but the United States Supreme Court did not agree. On the other hand, it did not entirely disagree, and thereby hangs the tale of the *Darlington* case[6] decided in 1965 and still the leading case on the subject of the role of section 8(a)(3) in plant closings.

Darlington Manufacturing Company operated a textile mill in Darlington, South Carolina. In March 1956, the Textile Workers Union began an organizing campaign among the company's employees. The company (in the language of the Supreme Court) "resisted vigorously." This resistance, among other things, included threats that the mill would be closed if the union were to win the NLRB representation election it was seeking.

The election was held on September 6, and the union won by 6 votes out of the 510 votes cast. Six days later, at a special meeting called by Darlington's president, Roger Milliken, Darlington's board of directors voted to liquidate the company and to call a special meeting of stockholders to that end. The stockholders meeting was held on October 17, the stockholders approved the dissolution, and the process of going out of business began at once. Production was halted on November 24, and the plant's machinery and equipment were sold at auction on December 12 and 13. The chronology is worth noting, because the speed of the Darlington dissolution was in marked contrast to the glacial progress of the NLRB case which began soon thereafter and which, one way or another, was in and out of the Board and the courts for the next twenty years.

Following the union's certification as bargaining agent by the Board on October 24, the union sought to bargain with Darlington, but its efforts were fruitless, and it filed charges with the NLRB. The charges alleged that Darlington violated the Act by (a) closing the plant in reprisal for union activity, and (b) failing to bargain at the union's request.[7]

Six years later, following an almost incredible series of legal maneuverings, the Board issued its decision. Meanwhile, it had remanded the case several times to its hearing officer to take additional testimony sought by the union, and the company had been in and out of court trying to enjoin the Board's actions. The evidence which the union wanted in the record was evidence which would link Darlington's parent, Deering-Milliken (which operated twenty-six other plants through seventeen companies), to the unfair labor practices charged against Darlington, so that any order to reinstate Darlington workers and to reimburse them for lost wages would have (as the tort lawyers inelegantly put it) a "deep-pockets defendant" still in existence to satisfy the Board's order.

The Board found Darlington guilty as charged, and Deering-Milliken as well. It rejected Darlington's claim of an absolute right to go out of business, but it added, cautiously, that it found "independent reason" for rejecting Darlington's contention in the fact that Darlington was part of a larger entity (Deering-Milliken). Here we have the beginning of the argument that has made the word "chill" a special part of the language not only of labor relations, but of libel law, first amendment law, and a great deal else. Closing one of several plants, the Borard argued (thus stepping neatly around the "absolute right to shut down" argument) is an unfair labor practice, for it will have the effect of chilling unionization in the remaining plants.

The Board's order, in addition to the normal cease and desist provisions, sought back pay and the placing of the Darlington employees on a preferential hiring list at Deering-Milliken. On the appeal to the U.S. Court of Appeals for the Fourth Circuit, the union added a request (not made by the Board) that the court order Darlington to reopen the plant, in order to reemploy the terminated Darlington employees.

The U.S. Court of Appeals rejected this extraordinary request, along with the rest of the arguments of the union and the Board. It agreed entirely with Darlington's "absolute right" thesis, saying: "To go out of business *in toto,* or to discontinue it in part permanently at any time, we think was Darlington's absolute prerogative....[T]he power to close, even if spurred by unionization is not precluded by the Act."[8]

The Board and the union both appealed to the United States Supreme Court. The union, hard-lining to the end, continued to argue that there was no absolute right to go out of business, if the motivation was antiunion. The Board, however, backed off, saying in its brief that it "does not consider it necessary to argue" that point in view of its reliance on the multiplant "chilling effect" theory. The Supreme Court went along with the Board, rejecting the "absolute right" theory argued by the company and adopted by the Court of Appeals. But, on the issue of *total* closing (i.e., a going-out-of-business shutdown), the Court was firm and unequivocal: "We hold that so far as the Labor Act is concerned, an employer has the absolute right to terminate his entire business for any reason he pleases."[9]

When the closure is total—when the employer is prepared to incur all the consequences of going out of business—his reason (even if it be, in the Court's phrase, "vindictiveness toward the union") does not matter. When, however, the closure is only partial, his state of mind does matter. If the effect is to chill unionism and if he could reasonably have foreseen that effect, the partial shutdown constitutes an unfair labor practice under section 8(a)(3).[10]

The two "ifs" in the foregoing sentence are significant. They are preconditions, in the Supreme Court's view, to a finding of an unfair labor practice based on antiunion animus in a plant shutdown case, and the Supreme Court remanded the case for findings by the Board on those issues.[11] Meanwhile, the right to shut down completely continues to remain absolute, regardless of the employer's intention or state of mind. As the Court put it: "A proposition that a single businessman cannot choose to go out of business if he wants to would represent such a startling innovation that it should not be entertained without the clearest manifestation of legislative intent or unequivocal judicial precedent so construing the Labor Act. We find neither."[12]

We take our leave of *Darlington* for now, although what the Court had to say concerning the right to shut down will engage us again at a later point. We move now to a consideration of the operation of the Act's bargaining provisions in plant-closing cases, where there is much more scope for the Act to operate than in the antidiscrimination area of section 8(a)(3).

5. *The Employer's Duty to Bargain: An Overview and Some History*

We have earlier indicated that the Act's collective bargaining provisions come much closer to creating a "workers' right," as we have been using that term, than do the antidiscrimination provisions of the Act just discussed. We now enlarge on that point.

The collective bargaining provisions of the Act are embodied principally in two sections—8(a)(5) and 8(d)—both of which are quoted below. They impose on the employer a mandatory duty to bargain collectively with the union which represents his organized employees. He must bargain over "wages, hours, and other terms and conditions of employment."[13] While the words "wages" and "hours" have generally caused no problems of interpretation, the more expansive and less specific phrase "terms and conditions of employment" has caused a great deal of controversy. It has been (fairly continuously) expanded by the Board to the point where it now includes not just the "terms and conditions of employment," as those words are commonly understood, but also anything an employer may do *that could have impact* on "terms and conditions," including the fundamental management decision as to whether or not a job shall exist. By thus extending the scope of the employer's bargaining duty, the Board would inject unions deeply into the managerial decision-making process.

If the subject area embraced by the employer's duty to bargain over "terms and conditions of employment" can properly be extended to management decisions to close plants, then a significant workers' right in respect of the job—a right to participate, at least to some extent, in the decision-making process involving the continuation (or not) of that job—arises under the collective bargaining provisions of the Act. Such a right would exceed anything which so-called plant-closing laws envision, for   it would enable employees to influence plant-closing decisions, perhaps to bring about their modification or rescission, or, at the very least, to delay the implementation of such decisions while the bargaining process takes place and, perhaps, to extract a price for such implementation.

The examination of the law which follows is intended to help us to determine, as best we can, the status of workers' rights in plant-closing situations as those rights are implemented through the employer's mandatory duty to bargain. A close analysis of the cases also permits a forecast of the direction which Board and court decisions in this area are likely to take.

But the job is only half done at that point. We must also examine what has been said, particularly by the U.S. Supreme Court, concerning the impact on management of the steady expansion of its duty to bargain over its decisions. In particular, we must examine the constraints and costs which the bargaining duty imposes in plant-closing situations, as well as others. If the impact on management is significant, then the impact on the economy is also significant. The policy implications are even broader. Resistance to increased costs of operation is (as management sees it) a managerial imperative. When mandatory bargaining doctrines of the Board add to operating costs—and add to them *for unionized employers only*—then employers can be expected to resist. The resistance will take the form not only of stiffer positions at the bargaining table, but also of a disposition to get out of the unionized situation, if possible, or to avoid it in the first place by stronger opposition to unionization, or to not move into areas where unionization will be invited. Thus the doctrines of the Board can have impact on the ebb and flow of economic events far removed from the bargaining table and the Board's immediate area of concern.

We turn now to the bargaining provisions of the Act and, thereafter, to the cases interpreting them.

Section 8(a)(5) of the Act provides that it is an unfair labor practice for an employer "to refuse to bargain collectively with the representatives of his employees."[14]

Section 8(d) of the Act, added in 1947, undertakes to define the content of the bargaining obligation. It does so at length. In the part which is pertinent to our discussion at this point, it provides as follows:

> (d) For the purposes of this section [8], to bargain collectively is the performance of the mutual obligation of the employer and the representative of the employees to meet at reasonable times and confer in good faith with respect to wages, hours, and other terms and conditions of employment...but such obligtion does not compel either party to agree to a proposal or require the making of a concession.

To understand how—and to what extent—the mandatory bargaining obligation just described has become an instrumentality for the creation and enforcement of workers' rights in plant-closing situations, we must trace the historical development of the employer's duty to bargain, for by studying how it originated and how it has developed we are better able to judge where it is today and where it is likely to go.

The history of the interpretation and application of the provisions quoted above, particularly the one which appeared in the original Wagner Act as section 8(5), is a case study in the tendency of regulatory agencies to expand their reach. The story of how the duty to bargain got from what it was (or what Congress *thought* it was when it enacted the Wagner Act) to where it is today provides a fascinating tale. Consider how simple the obligation was thought to be by the Wagner Act's chief sponsor (aside from Senator Wagner himself) in the United States Senate in 1935: All the law proposes to do, said Senator Walsh, once a union has been chosen is "to escort them to the door of the employer and say, 'Here they are, the legal representatives of your employees.' What happens behind those doors is not inquired into, and the bill does not seek to inquire into it." It is almost a tautology these days to remark that the Board almost immediately set about making a liar out of Senator Walsh by engrafting on the bargaining duty the obligation that the bargaining be conducted "in good faith"—a qualification which instantly and dramatically thrust the Board right through that door and into the bargaining room. Even back then, some supporters of Senator Wagner's bill, notably Dr. George W. Taylor of the Wharton School at the University of Pennsylvania, a forthright and influential enthusiast for collective bargaining, thought that the bargaining unfair labor practice was naive, that a provision for mandatory bargaining could only get more and more complex and overrefined as time went on. Dr. Taylor urged that there be no section 8(5), but he was ignored. Later, when his fears became fact, he urged the repeal of section 8(a)(5), but again he was ignored.[15] The progress from Senator Walsh's simple concept to the Board's requirement that the employer bargain over his plant-closing *decision,* even before it is made, is, even in the history of regulatory expansiveness, something of a phenomenon.

Beginning early,[16] and with growing vigor over the past several decades, the National Labor Relations Board has been extending the range of subjects on which bargaining with unions is required. Correspondingly, the Board's overall thrust has been to reduce the decisional area in which management, once a union enters the picture, will be permitted to act unilaterally.[17] In consequence, the process of managerial decision making has become more complicated (and more costly) in unionized situations, as more and more subjects, once thought to be within the exclusive province of management, have been thrown into the bargaining process. Decisions concerning the locus of operations, and their continuation, discontinuation, or removal (although these are by no means the only managerial areas involved in the Board's duty-to-bargain doctrine) are highly relevant examples for our purposes. As will be seen in the discussion of the case law which follows, there is significant tension (sometimes explicit, sometimes not) between the managerial imperative to operate efficiently and to react in timely and responsive fashion to economic circumstances, on the one hand, and the bargaining rights of unions and their members on the other.

Stated more simply, the issue (one which we have already seen in the *Darlington* case) is one of workers' rights versus management rights reduced to this: to what extent did Congress intend (to what extent *could* Congress, constitutionally, attempt) to subordinate property rights and their incidents, including the right and responsibility of management to manage its assets effectively, to a policy of expanding and protecting employee rights and promoting collective bargaining?

As will appear from the discussion which follows, every worker right has a cost to the employer in some respect—usually either in money or efficiency—and the policy consideration underlying it all is, how much of such cost is legitimate? How much did Congress intend? How much is too much in a market economy? The Board has traditionally seen the Act as overriding. Some courts, including the U.S. Supreme Court, have disagreed and refused to go as far as the Board has urged. Occasionally, the Board has been turned back or corrected by the courts as it advanced toward its policy goals; at other times, the courts have tended to defer to the Board's presumed expertise in labor-management affairs, although this seems to be less so when the central issue is *management* and its rights and problems. There the courts seem to feel that their own expertise is as good as the Board's, perhaps better.

One result of all this has been the development of an elaborate set of rules concerning how an employer must conduct himself in collective bargaining if he is not to be vulnerable to a charge that he has not bargained "in good faith"—a concept which, as we earlier remarked, was engrafted on the Wagner Act by the Board and which was subsequently embodied in the Taft-Hartley Act's definition of the duty to bargain collectively quoted above. The penalties on an employer can be substantial if he has an obligation to bargain wtih the union in respect of a particular managerial action and he fails, in the opinion of the Board, to fulfill it. Aside from the heavy cost involved in litigation before the Board, and possibly later in the courts, the employer can be forced to pay a heavy price in complying with remedial orders of the Board. He may, for example, be required, as we shall see, to reinstitute a discontinued operation and reinstate, with back pay, its former employees.

For an employer faced with a shutdown decision, therefore, it has become critical to know (1) whether he has a bargaining obligation, and (2) if so, what it is and how can it be fulfilled. For example, does good faith bargaining require, in a particular situation, advance notice to the union of a projected management action? Notice only, or notice plus bargaining? And, if bargaining is required, is the bargaining to be only over the *impact* of the decision on employees or is it to be over the very decision itself, *before it is actually made?*

These are the issues with which the cases that follow are concerned, and one aim of this study is to provide some guidance as to where the law now stands, or appears to stand, and where it seems likely to go in the future in respect of workers' rights and management rights in plant-closing situations.

IV. Decision Bargaining—The Early Cases

1. *The* Fibreboard *Case*

Although the *Fibreboard* case[1] did not involve plant closure (it was, as we shall see, a contracting-out case), the principles enunciated in *Fibreboard* are important because in that case (1) the Supreme Court accepted the Board's theory of "decision bargaining"—at least on the facts before it, and (2) the distinction between the duty to bargain over the *effects* of a management decision and a duty to bargain over the *decision itself* was intrinsic to the Court's ruling. There is wide agreement that bargaining over "effects" (i.e., measures to cushion the impact of a management decision on the employees affected by it, especially when they are dislocated) is a salutary labor relations practice. There is no such consensus, however, concerning decision bargaining, i.e., mandatory bargaining *before a decision is taken,* over the question of whether or not it will be taken and implemented. Indeed, the concept of decision bargaining (although it did not make its appearance until the Board was almost thirty years old) has proved to be one of the Board's most controversial doctrines.

Its rationale is surprisingly simple. It is that the right to bargain over terms of employment *must* include the right to bargain over the most fundamental term of all: the existence of the job. Stated that way, it will seem to many to be simple, logical—and unobjectionable. Employers see it, however, as anything but logical and certainly objectionable. The entire thrust of the Act—its representation provisions, as well as its bargaining provisions—they argue, is predicated on the assumption that an employment relationship already exists, and it is certainly true that the rights conferred by the Act are conferred upon "employees." Accordingly, it is argued that the decision as to whether or not a job should exist, or continue to exist, is for management and management alone, for it involves the most fundamental of management functions: the determination of what needs to be done, by what type of worker, and at what location or locations. Management alone (management argues) has the responsibility, on behalf of the owners of the business, to make these decisions and to make them in the best interests of the enterprise. That decision-making function cannot be shared with unions (or, for that matter, with anyone else who has no responsibility for the success of the enterprise and no ownership stake in its survival). Thus, greatly abbreviated, runs the employer argument.

In one sense, that argument (sound though it might be in terms of property rights and entrepreneurial economics) was, by the time of the *Fibreboard* case, rather anachronistic. The Board might have argued in reply (although it never bothered to) that the fundamental rights of management to manage the enterprise were massively invaded by the Act when it was passed with its limitations on employer freedom to hire and fire, fix wages and hours, and so forth. The employers' quarrel, therefore, was with the Congress, rather than the Board. Such an argument would, however, have been a little disingenuous, for the fact is that never before had there been quite so bold an incursion into the management area as the Board's theory that the congressionally-imposed duty to bargain included a mandatory duty to bargain over management decisions—that the right of the union to bargain (or to be bargained with) included a right to participate to that extent in the decision-making process itself. Whatever had existed before in the way of workers' rights, the decision-bargaining doctrine clearly spelled out a right which went to the very heart of the employment relationship. In consequence, decision bargaining was a hot topic in labor-management circles long before the *Fibreboard* case got to the United States Supreme Court.

The case has an interesting history. It is worth digressing to recount that history because of the light it sheds on how politics affect the ebb and flow of the Board's decisional policies, including, as we shall later see, its policies relating to plant closing and workers' rights. It also furnishes an example of the tendency of those policies, in general and over time, to develop in directions favorable to the expansion of union bargaining power, including enabling unions to intervene, through the statutory bargaining process, in management decisions involving plant closures. When that tendency (coupled with the Board's disposition to try to minimize the impact of court decisions on its policies[2]) is taken into account, the decisions of the Board are both more understandable and more predictable.

Fibreboard first came before the Board in 1961 on a complaint by a local of the Steelworkers Union that the company had violated its duty to bargain by not negotiating with the union over its decision to contract out certain maintenance operations which had theretofore been performed by members of the union. These union members were laid off in consequence of the contracting out.[3] Fibreboard had, for some time, been concerned over the high cost of its operations. Some of its other unions apparently had shown a willingness to discuss a solution to the problem, but the complaining union had refused. Thereafter, Fibreboard investigated the possibilities of contracting out its maintenance services, having been advised that it could thereby effect economies in manpower, fringe benefits, and overtime costs. Some months before its contract with the complaining union was up for renegotiation, the union served notice of its readiness to negotiate a new agreement. The company did not respond until shortly before the contract's expiration date, at which time it informed the union that it had determined that substantial savings could be achieved by contracting out the maintenance services, and it added, in a letter to the union, that "In these circumstances, we are sure you will realize that negotiation of a new contract would be pointless."[4]

Thereafter, the union filed charges of refusal to bargain under section 8(a)(5) and of antiunion discrimination under section 8(a)(3). The refusal-to-bargain charge was based on the then novel theory that the employer's bargaining obligation under section 8(a)(5) included a duty to bargain over the contracting-out *decision*—and to do so before the decision was made—and that the employer's failure to afford the union an opportunity for such bargaining constituted a failure to bargain in good faith. Thus, the issue of decision bargaining was posed. The administrative law judge before whom the case was tried rejected the decision-bargaining theory and found no other merit in the 8(a)(5) charge or in the 8(a)(3) charge. The Board agreed with him. On the section 8(a)(5) issue, the Board held that employment itself (i.e., whether or not a job shall exist) could not be a bargainable condition of employment, and then expressed the view that Congress never intended "to compel bargaining concerning basic management decisions, such as whether and to what extent to risk capital and managerial effort."[5] And there the matter rested—briefly.

Soon the Board's personnel and its decisional doctrine began to reflect the election in 1960 of President John F. Kennedy, and the fact that his administration's philosophy with respect to organized labor was different from that of President Dwight D. Eisenhower's. A year after the Board's decision in *Fibreboard I* had been handed down, what came to be known as the Kennedy Board handed down a decision in the *Town & Country* case.[6] Departing from the philosophy which had guided the "Eisenhower Board" majority in *Fibreboard I*, the "Kennedy Board" now laid down a different rule, which became the cornerstone of the decision-bargaining doctrine. The theory and the rationale underlying it were explained in *Town & Country* as follows:

> This obligation to bargain [over the management decision, in advance] in nowise restrains an employer from formulating or effectuating an economic decision to terminate a phase of his business operations. Nor does it obligate him to yield to a union's demand that a subcontract not be let, or that it be let on terms inconsistent with management's business judgment. Experience has shown, however, that candid discussion of mutual problems by labor and management frequently results in their resolution with attendant benefit to both sides. Business operations may profitably continue and jobs may be preserved. Such prior discussion with a duly designated bargaining representative is all that the Act contemplates. But it commands no less.[7]

The reader will notice the apparent inconsistency, in the excerpt just quoted, between the Board's assurances that all that is required under the new theory is "discussion," and the imposition in the next breath ("it *commands* no less") of the *mandatory* duty to bargain (with all that duty implies in terms not only of compulsion, but also of the Board's standards of "good faith," the employer's exposure to possible strike action, and the always touchy question of when the duty to bargain has been legally discharged by virtue of an "impasse").

Following *Town & Country,* the Kennedy Board moved to reconsider the year-old decision of its predecessor in *Fibreboard I,* maneuvering the case back before it for rehearing. This time the result was different. In *Fibreboard II,* the new Board majority, relying on *Town & Country,* reversed *Fibreboard I* and held that the company had indeed violated its obligations under the Act by not having engaged in decision bargaining before contracting out its maintenance services.[8]

The Board's new bargaining requirements were challenged by one of its holdover members. Member Ray Rodgers, in a strong dissenting opinion, expressed his concern over the new direction in which the Board was steering collective bargaining:

> If this ruling of the majority stands, it is difficult to foresee any economic action which management will be free to take of its own volition and in its own vital interest (whether it be the discontinuance of an unprofitable line, *the closing of an unnecessary facility,* or the abandonment of an outmoded procedure) which would not be the subject of mandatory bargaining.[9]

That, of course, was very much the philosophy of the Kennedy Board implemented, as we shall see, in a variety of situations. The damage that dissenting Board Member Rodgers foresaw was controlled somewhat by the concurring opinion, discussed below, of Justice Potter Stewart when the *Fibreboard* case got to the Supreme Court. But the tension between union and management interests set up in the *Town & Country* and *Fibreboard* line of cases continues to plague the case law to this day—especially as the bargaining obligation has been extended beyond the contracting-out issue involved in those cases to a broad range of other management decisions, including plant closings—precisely as anticipated by Member Rodgers in his dissent in *Fibreboard II:* "In the final analysis, the subjecting of such management decisions as this to the ambit of the Board's processes, and particularly to the mandatory bargaining requirements, simply means that, short of complete union agreement, any action taken by management must hereafter be taken at its peril."[10]

An examination of the *process* which the Board employed in establishing its decision-bargaining doctrine is worth brief notice at this point, not so much by way of a study in administrative technique (although it is that), but because it helps to explain the sometimes unsteady progress of the law in this area. Taking a case in which the situation (contracting out) was about as amenable to the bargaining process as wages or hours (indeed, the contracting out in *Fibreboard* largely turned on those very issues), the Board used it as a basis for laying down a rule of mandatory bargaining which is of much broader potential application, as the foregoing quotation from the dissent of Member Rodgers indicates. When applied in other, more difficult circumstances (such as a decision over a plant closing), the bargaining, predictably, is found to be far less likely to result in mutual accommodation. This is because in plant-closing situations the interests and positions of the parties do not merely *differ* (as in wage negotiations) but are usually in complete conflict. The Kennedy Board majority seemed unaware of that practical problem and of such considerations as these: Under what circumstances can a union be expected to concur in a decision which will abolish its members' jobs and probably cost the union both members and dues? At what point in a negotiation—and at what cost—will a compromise be negotiated? Does not giving the union a right to bargain over decisions concerning (as the pre-Kennedy Board put it in *Fibreboard I*) "to what extent to risk capital and managerial effort" confer upon the union significant power over the deployment of the firm's assets? At what point in a negotiation over a plant-closure decision can management safely assume that the Board will hold that it has fulfilled its bargaining obligations, that a legal impasse has been reached, and that it is, therefore, free to proceed unilaterally?

That the problems posed by the decision-bargaining doctrine are not merely theoretical and that the risk is quite real is shown by the remedy prescribed by the Board in *Fibreboard II* (and approved by the Supreme Court): the Board ordered Fibreboard to reinstitute its maintenance operations, to reinstate with back pay the employees previously engaged in those operations, and then to proceed to fulfill its bargaining obligation with the union.

The relevance of that sort of remedy to a study of plant-closure situations hardly requires elaboration. By imposing the potential for such heavy costs in the event of an adverse decision, the Board influences the judgment of management *and* unions, perhaps deterring an otherwise necessary and justifiable shutdown by management, perhaps inducing a union to "hang tough" and offer no ameliorating concessions if bargaining over the shutdown does take place, in hopes that it can prevail before the Board and thereby undo the entire management decision. On the other hand, as in any other litigation, the prospects of losing it all may operate to cause the parties to come to an accommodation. If not ruinously costly, such an accommodation might allow management to do what it must, while providing some compensatory cushion for the affected employees.

Fibreboard II quickly made its way to the Supreme Court,[11] the United States Court of Appeals for the District of Columbia having agreed completely with the Board that mandatory bargaining over the contracting-out decision was required as a means of affording the union "an opportunity to meet management's legitimate complaints" concerning its costs.[12] The principal opinion in the Supreme Court was written by Chief Justice Earl Warren, with a strong concurring opinion by Justice Stewart, in which he was joined by Justices William O. Douglas and John Marshall Harlan.

The opinions in the Supreme Court are worth examining in some detail. Although the case deals with contracting out rather than plant closure, it is clear that Justice Stewart saw it correctly (as NLRB Member Rodgers had) as having much broader implications—as, in fact, potentially extending over a broad range of management decisions, including plant closings—and so did the other federal courts (including, ultimately, the Supreme Court itself) in cases dealing with the nature and scope of management's obligation to bargain over plant-closing decisions.

We turn first to the majority opinion of Chief Justice Warren, which stated the issues as follows:

First, is there a duty to bargain "about whether to let to an independent contractor for legitimate business reasons" work which had previously been performed by employees of the employer. (The phrase "whether to let" squarely poses the decision-bargaining issue, although it is by no means clear from the rest of the opinion that the Chief Justice was entirely aware of what the term implied.)

Second, was the Board empowered under the Act—given that the case involved only a refusal to bargain under section 8(a)(5) and not antiunion animus and discriminatory conduct under section 8(a)(3)—to order Fibreboard to resume its discontinued operations and to offer reinstatement and back pay to the employees displaced by the contracting out?[13]

The Court answered both questions in the affirmative.[14] In doing so, it rejected the argument (which had figured in the case from the outset and had been explicitly embraced by the Eisenhower Board) that whether or not the job shall exist at all is *not* one of the "terms and conditions of employment" over which bargaining is required under section 8(d) of the Act. "The words [terms and conditions]," said the Chief Justice, "plainly cover termination of employment which, as the facts of this case indicate, necessarily results from the contracting out of work."[15]

The Court spent considerable time documenting the bargainability of contracting out. To a large extent, this would seem to have been unnecessary, even arguably irrelevant. The issue was not whether subcontracting as a business practice could be (and is, on occasion) bargained about, but whether a *management decision* to do it *must* be bargained about before the fact. The Chief Justice's opinion, while responding to that issue in the affirmative, offered little in the way of argumentation in support of the *theory* of decision bargaining itself. At times, it almost appears as if the Chief Justice did not quite grasp the radical sweep of the Board's new doctrine.[16] Justice Stewart, on the other hand, clearly did understand the new doctrine and was determined to define its limits, as we shall see.

The closest the Chief Justice came to indicating limits to the application of his ruling—that is, areas in which decision bargaining might not be required—was in his stress on the facts of the case before him and in his taking pains to note (in support of the Court's ruling) that:

(1) No issue of capital investment was involved;

(2) To require the employer to bargain about replacing his employees with others to do the same work "would not significantly abridge his freedom to manage the business"; and

(3) The kinds of things that Fibreboard was seeking to obtain by contracting out (economies in manpower, fringe costs, and overtime) are peculiarly suitable for collective bargaining.[17]

From those cautious remarks, it is perhaps not unwarranted to anticipate that the Court would decide otherwise in a case involving capital investment, or freedom to manage the enterprise, or other subject matter deemed less appropriate to the bargaining process. And indeed it did—in the *First National Maintenance* case in 1981, to which we shall shortly be coming. That Justice Stewart would have decided such a different case differently is abundantly clear from his concurring opinion. Because that opinion has become so much of a touchstone for other judges, we examine it in some detail.

Although the principal opinion was hedged, it was apparently not enough for Justice Stewart, who opened his concurring opinion by stating that the decision still "radiates implications of such disturbing breadth" as to force him to speak out.[18] He therefore begins by confirming what the case does *not* decide: "The Court most assuredly does not decide that every managerial decision which necessarily terminates an individual's employment is subject to the duty to bargain. Nor does the Court decide that subcontracting decisions are as a general matter subject to that duty."[19]

He then turns to what is, for him, the heart of the matter: the freedom to make managerial decisions versus the duty to bargain over "conditions of employment" (in other words, the workers' rights/management rights dichotomy). He concedes that the case probably has put to rest the argument that "whether there is to be a job is not a condition of employment," and he therefore agrees that employment security is a legitimate "condition of employment." But he quickly adds that "it surely does not follow that every decision which may affect job security is a subject of compulsory collective bargaining."[20] Elaborating on these points, Justice Stewart notes that there are "areas in which decisions by management may quite clearly imperil job security, or indeed terminate it entirely," giving as examples (1) a decision to invest in labor-saving machinery, and (2) a decision to liquidate assets and go out of business. As to such decisions, Justice Stewart then says: "Nothing the Court holds today should be understood as imposing a duty to bargain collectively regarding such managerial decisions, which lie at the core of entrepreneurial control."[21] He goes on in language which, like the foregoing, is quoted repeatedly in subsequent cases:

> Decisions concerning the commitment of investment capital or the basic scope of the enterprise are not in themselves primarily about conditions of employment, though the effect of the decision may necessarily be to terminate employment. If, as I think clear, the purpose of Section 8(d) is

to describe a limited area subject to the duty of collective bargaining, those management decisions which are fundamental to the basic direction of a corporate enterprise or which impinge only indirectly upon employment security should be excluded from that area.[22]

Having laid down his limiting principles, Justice Stewart then states that he does not believe that subcontracting practices in general are "conditions of employment," but on the particular facts in *Fibreboard* (where "all that is involved is the substitution of one group of workers for another to perform the same tasks in the same plant under the ultimate control of the same employer"), he sees the situation as closely analogous to questions of discharge and work assignment, seniority and retirement, about which compulsory bargaining is commonplace.

Returning, however, once again to his major preoccupation, he adds:

> This kind of subcontracting falls short of such larger entrepreneurial questions as what shall be produced, how capital shall be invested in fixed assets, or what the basic scope of the enterprise shall be. In my view, the Court's decision in this case has nothing to do with whether any aspects of those larger issues could under any circumstances be considered subjects of compulsory collective bargaining under the present law.[23]

It is perhaps worth remarking at this point that, up to now, we have devoted much time (and shall be devoting more) to various aspects of workers' rights. Justice Stewart, while by no means insensitive, as his opinion shows, to such rights, reminds us that there are also entrepreneurial rights (we have elsewhere referred to them as "management rights") which need to be considered. The reminder is a healthy one. As we shall see, it led the Court in a subsequent case to attempt a balancing between the two sets of rights.

We conclude by returning, briefly, to the opinion of the Chief Justice for the Court's decision on the issue of the *remedy* prescribed by the Board. It will be recalled that the Board's order required Fibreboard (notwithstanding the admittedly economic motivation of the company and the absence of any element of antiunion animus) to rescind its decision and reinstitute the maintenance operations which had been contracted out, to reinstate the displaced employees with back pay, and to proceed thereafter to bargain, as required, over its subcontracting decision. It was argued by the company that an order to revoke the managerial decision and restore the *status quo* exceeded the Board's remedial power, that, in the absence of charges of discrimination against employees under section 8(a)(3), it was not appropriate to command their reinstatement. But the entire Court found the remedy to be well within the administrative discretion confided to the Board by the Act and not an "undue or unfair burden on the Company."

As we indicated earlier, the implications of this remedy for plant-closure situations are both obvious and serious. It seemed possible, nevertheless, after the *Fibreboard* decision, that the impact of the Board's decision-bargaining doctrine might be blunted by (1) the stress which both opinions in the Supreme Court laid on the confinement of the *Fibreboard* decision to its particular facts, and (2) Justice Stewart's explicit and emphatic concern for managerial control and flexibility and his careful listing of the situations in which the *Fibreboard* decision would *not* apply. That possibility quickly evaporated, as we shall see. The Board ignored Justice Stewart's opinion entirely and refused to see Chief Justice Warren's opinion as placing any significant limits on its decision-bargaining theory.

2. *After* Fibreboard: *The Tussle between the Board and the Courts of Appeal*

It was almost twenty years before the Supreme Court again addressed itself to decision bargaining and, when it did, it was in a plant-closing case. In that case (*First National Maintenance,* decided in 1981), the Supreme Court laid down definitive rules for decision bargaining in plant-closing cases and indicated guidelines for the imposition of the decision-bargaining duty in general.

We cannot fully appreciate what the court did in *First National Maintenance,* however, without viewing it against the background of certain key decisions rendered by the Board and the federal appellate courts in the intervening years. To a large extent that background discloses an almost continuous struggle between a Board anxious to consolidate what it saw as a victory in *Fibreboard* for the decision-bargaining principle, and a federal judiciary not prepared to embrace that doctrine quite so enthusiastically.

The first case, *Adams Dairy,* began even before the Supreme Court handed down its decision in the *Fibreboard* case. In *Adams Dairy,* the company decided to change its method of operation from delivery of its products by its own drivers to delivery by an independent contractor. (To relate the factual situation in *Adams* to our preoccupation here, it might be said that what Adams did was roughly analogous to partial discontinuance of operations.) The Board issued a *Fibreboard*-type order (reinstatement of the operation and the employees with back pay),[24] but the Court of Appeals for the Eighth Circuit refused to enforce the Board's order.[25] The Board appealed to the Supreme Court, but the Court remanded the case for reconsideration in the light of its intervening decision in *Fibreboard*.[26] The Eighth Circuit reconsidered, but hewed firmly to its original view, buttressed now by language from Justice Stewart's concurring opinion in *Fibreboard*.

The Court of Appeals reasoned that the case did not involve a mere substitution of one set of employees for another (as did *Fibreboard*) but a basic change in operations, a kind of partial liquidation, and a change in capital structure and investment—all of which echoed the reasoning of Justice Stewart.[27] The Eighth Circuit even found support in the opinion of Chief Justice Warren in *Fibreboard*, which had said that to compel decision bargaining in that case would *not* "significantly abridge" the employer's "freedom to manage the business," whereas in the *Adams* case the Court of Appeals thought it would.

Between its first and second decisions in *Adams Dairy*, the same court reached a similar result in a quite different sort of case—one involving not contracting out, but the closure of a branch operation because of total loss of its customers.[28]

The Burns Detective Agency provides, among other things, security guards for plants and other installations and institutions. The union had been certified as bargaining representative for the Burns guards in the Omaha area in February 1963. Before negotiations could commence, however, Burns lost its last customer (Creighton University) for guard services in that area, and it so advised the union in April, adding that, under the circumstances (no contract for services, no need for guards, no justification for a branch office), there seemed to be "no practical reason for meeting" to discuss a contract to cover the defunct operation. The union responded by filing charges with the Board.

After some preliminary confusion as to how to proceed against Burns, the Board settled on a charge of refusal to bargain with the union over the management decision to terminate the contract between Burns and its customer, Creighton University, and the consequent shutdown of its Omaha branch. The Board issued a decision ordering Burns to bargain with the union.[29] The Eighth Circuit Court of Appeals refused to enforce the Board's order, holding that there had been no improper failure to bargain, because, unlike Fibreboard, Burns "completely discontinued" its Omaha operation—no contracting out was involved.[30] Justice Stewart is quoted at length concerning the "narrower concept" of "conditions of employment" for which he had argued in *Fibreboard,* and his language to the effect that not every decision that may affect job security is thereby made a subject of compulsory collective bargaining is set forth at length, as is his strong affirmation of the right of management to be free of an obligation to bargain over managerial decisions "which lie at the core of entrepreneurial control."

But the greater significance of the *Burns* case—a partial closing situation—lies in the court's introduction of the *Darlington* case. Noting the absence of antiunion animus, the court said that the "teaching" of *Darlington* is that "partial closing of one's business is not an unfair labor practice in the absence of a showing of motivation which is aimed at achieving a prohibited result." The court applied *Darlington* to decision bargaining in these words:

> Under *Darlington*, the finding of lack of anti-union motivation in closing the Omaha division for economic reasons precludes a finding of unfair labor practice in refusing to bargain with the Union on the cancellation of the Creighton contract and the closing of the Omaha division.[31]

What the Eighth Circuit is here attributing to the Supreme Court in *Darlington* is an idea which was strongly implied in the *Darlington* opinion: when the action of an employer in closing out *part* of an operation is free of antiunion animus (or similar illicit motivation), it is *altogether* free of the Act. The same considerations which impelled the Court in *Darlington* to recognize the "*absolute right* [of the operator of a business] to terminate his *entire* business for any reasons he pleases" (emphasis added)[32] apply as well, says the Eighth Circuit, to the termination of *part* of the business when there is no invidious motivation for doing so. To put it another way, the two courts (the Eighth Circuit explicitly, the Supreme Court implicitly) reject the Board's theory that the Act transcends (and the employee rights created by it take precedence over) the inherent and traditional property rights of the owner of a business in respect of the closing of one of his plants.

The Eighth Circuit Court of Appeals reaffirmed its view several years later in *Morrison Cafeterias*.[33] In the *Morrison* case, the union won an election at the company's Little Rock cafeteria. That evening the Little Rock employees were informed that the operation was being shut down, but that they would be offered employment elsewhere, and they were, a few days later. Neither the shutdown nor the offer of other employment was negotiated with the union, although, in between the two actions, the union demanded negotiations. When its demand was not complied with, it filed charges with the Board.[34]

At first the Board proceeded against Morrison on the basis of a discriminatory shutdown in violation of section 8(a)(3). It found Morrison guilty, but while the case was on appeal the Board asked the Eighth Circuit to remand the case for reconsideration in light of the *Darlington* case. On remand, the board's administrative law judge saw the case as involving both *Darlington* and *Fibreboard*. As to the first, he found that Morrison, like Darlington, had shut down to avoid doing business with the union, but he exonerated Morrison on the ground that, unlike Darlington, the "partial closing"—the shutdown of the single cafeteria—was not motivated by an intention to "chill unionism" in the other parts of the operation.[35] On the *Fibreboard* (decision bargaining) issue, he found that Morrison had violated section 8(a)(5) by failing to notify the union and failing to bargain over both the decision and the effects of the closing. The Eighth Circuit, however, again refused to enforce the Board's decision-bargaining order, and it did so citing *Darlington* again. This time the court was able to rely on the views of a member of the NLRB. It quoted at length from the opinion written by Member Sam Zagoria, who, dissenting from the holding of the Board majority in the *Morrison* case, had argued that when there is no motive to "chill unionism" a refusal-to-bargain finding is "completely foreclosed" by *Darlington*.[36]

Nevertheless, the court did decide to require bargaining over the *effects* of the decision to close. It acknowledged that its decision was, to that extent, interfering with the exercise of the right to shut down, but said that "*Darlington* recognizes the need to balance employer and employee rights."[37]

Balancing of that sort, however, was not what the Board had in mind as it pressed on with the implementation of its collective bargaining philosophy, notwithstanding the opposition it encountered in other circuits besides the Eighth. Indeed, the Board's persistence in the face of judicial disapproval has been, for much of its existence, a noteworthy characteristic of the agency, doing little for stability and predictability in NLRB matters. The knowledge by a litigant, for example, that he may lose before the Board and yet prevail ultimately before a court—or that he may win before the Board but lose in the court proceeding to enforce the Board's order—or that a majority of a sitting Board may soon be superseded by a majority which may hold differently on his issue—makes decision making vexatious and can translate into substantial costs.

The Third U.S. Court of Appeals had before it in 1965 (the same year
in which the Eighth Circuit decided *Adams* and *Burns*) the case of *Royal
Plating & Polishing Co.*[38] The company's decision (not bargained about)
to shut down one of its two plants called forth the usual Board order to
revoke the action, reinstate the employees, and bargain over the decision
and its impact on the employees. The Third Court of Appeals refused to
enforce the Board's order, holding that the decision to shut down was an
investment decision involving a change in economic direction. That being
so, the decision was not subject to bargaining, because (quoting Justice
Stewart) it lay "at the core of entrepreneurial control." The Board also
fared badly on similar reasoning by the Ninth U.S. Court of Appeals two
years later,[39] and by the Tenth Circuit two years after that.[40]

3. *The* Ozark Trailers *Case: The NLRB on Workers' Rights*

We come now to the case which in some respects represents, to the
Board's advocates and opponents alike, the high-water mark of the
Board's campaign to establish its philosophy with respect to the
employer's duty to bargain in shutdown situations. Consequently,
although *Ozark Trailers* was decided earlier than most of the post-
Fibreboard cases we have been discussing, it provides an appropriate
conclusion to this phase of our discussion.[41]

Ozark Trailers, Inc., a manufacturer of refrigerated truck bodies, had
a contract with a union. During the term of the contract, Ozark closed its
only plant without consulting the union. The case might thus be thought
to be a simple one: neither *Darlington* nor *Fibreboard* would hold the
Act to be applicable to what appeared to be a going-out-of-business decision at a single plant. But the Board approached it differently. First, taking a leaf from *Darlington,* it held that *Ozark* was not a single plant but
rather one of three corporations engaged in integrated operations that
were, therefore, a single employer for purposes of the Act. Then, shifting
to *Fibreboard,* it held that such a "partial closing" required, under that
case, notice to the union and bargaining, both over the decision and over
its effects. Ozark did not appeal the order, and so the Board's decision
stands as issued.[42]

Ozark Trailers is important on several counts. In addition to what it
reveals concerning the Board's tenacity on the issue of decision bargaining, the case makes explicit the Board's own theory of workers' rights
versus management rights. In *Ozark Trailers* the Board argues that there
is a right on the part of the worker in his job, which arises out of simply
having worked at the job over time. In the Board's view, that right

equates with the traditional ownership rights of investors in their capital. Here, surely, is a sweeping statement of some sort of job rights principle. The Board argues it this way (elbowing Justice Stewart aside as it goes):

> [W]e do not believe that the question of whether a particular management decision must be bargained about should turn on whether the decision involves the commitment of invested capital or on whether it may be characterized as involving [a] 'major' or 'basic' change in the nature of the employer's business. True it is that decisions of this nature are, by definition, of significance for the employer. It is equally true, however, and ought not be lost sight of, that an employer's decision to make a 'major' change in the nature of his business, such as the termination of a portion thereof, is also of significance for those employees whose jobs will be lost by the termination. *For, just as the employer has invested capital in the business, so the employee has invested years of his working life, accumulating seniority, accruing pension rights, and developing skills that may or may not be saleable to another employer. And, just as the employer's interest in the proliferation of his capital investment is entitled to consideration in our interpretation of the Act, so too is the employee's interest in the protection of his livelihood.* (Emphasis added.)[43]

Thus the Board not only reaffirmed its belief in decision bargaining—and in terms which brought it squarely into conflict with the courts—but it also devised a new concept to support it. The "employee's interest in the protection of his livelihood" (which comes very close to defining a "worker's right") is offered as a justification for requiring bargaining over management decisions which may affect the employee's livelihood. Further emphasizing its preference for workers' rights (as against property rights or management rights), the Board, in the above excerpt, dismisses "the commitment of invested capital" or making a "major" or "basic" change in the business as controlling considerations. In its view, those are *not* the factors on which "the question of whether a particular management decision must be bargained about should turn." As we shall shortly be seeing, this rationale was explicitly rejected by the Supreme Court in the *First National Maintenance* case, but that decision was still five years away when the Board was deciding *Ozark Trailers*.

The Board did a good deal more in the *Ozark Trailers* case. Perhaps seeking to make its mandatory decision-bargaining philosophy more palatable, the Board went on to define the actual bargaining obligation so "softly" as to be in some respects hardly recognizable by practitioners in the labor-management field. The employer's duty to bargain, said the

Board reassuringly, is only a duty to "discuss" his intentions with the union which represents his employees. Now in labor relations parlance, among professionals in the field, "discussion" means no more than that term ordinarily implies. It does *not* mean *bargaining* and certainly not *mandatory* bargaining. Yet mandatory bargaining is precisely what the Board is talking about. Was it ignorant of the distinction, known to any tyro in the field, between mere "discussion" and "mandatory bargaining"? Possibly. As we elsewhere remark,[44] the Board (notwithstanding its official status as the expert government agency in labor relations) has never shown a very good grasp of day-to-day labor-management affairs. More likely, however, the Board in *Ozark Trailers* was simply being disingenuous.

The Board went on in *Ozark Trailers* to offer still further reassurances to management—but ultimately they were to prove no more reliable than its soft definition of the mandatory bargaining obligation. If the "discussion" fails to produce agreement, said the Board, "the employer is wholly free to make and effectuate his decision." Some years later, however, that turned out to be spectacularly untrue. An employer who fully discharged his decision-bargaining obligation was held by the Board *not* to have the right to move ahead to "effectuate his decision."[45] Was the Board deliberately misleading in *Ozark*? Probably not. It simply had a different fish to fry. It was trying to make decision bargaining seem more reasonable and less of a threat to management than it appeared to many management observers at the time to be.[46]

But it fell short of that objective, even in *Ozark Trailers,* for it went on to advance a view which, once again, ran counter to experience and common sense among labor relations professionals—at least those on the management side. It was "no significant intrusion" on the right to run the business, the Board said, "to require that an employer—once he has reached the point of thinking seriously about taking such an extraordinary step as relocating or terminating a portion of his business—to discuss that step with the bargaining representative of the employees who will be affected by his decision."[47]

To any professional who ever sat on either side of the bargaining table, that statement is palpable nonsense, especially in light of the fact that what the Board is blandly describing as mere "discussion" is, in reality, a *compulsory* requirement to engage in negotiations with a union until either agreement or (what the Board will regard as) impasse is reached. It is, in point of fact, an enormous "intrusion" to require that critical business decisions be submitted to the bargaining process before they can be made and implemented.[48] It may be an intrusion which is justifiable in some way, or on some nonbusiness criterion, but an intrusion it surely is. So the question is not whether there is a "significant intrusion" or not, but whether such an intrusion can be justified. Ought management rights to be subordinated, as a matter of national policy, to employee rights and union rights? And, if so, did Congress incorporate that policy in the Act? The Board plainly thought so, on both counts, as it demonstrated again and again. Others (including, as we shall see, the United States Supreme Court) are less certain.

In sum, the decisions in the *Fibreboard* line of cases which we have been reviewing disclose a consistent objective on the part of the Board to extend the mandatory bargaining obligation as broadly as possible—arguably, beyond anything that the Congress could have had in mind when it enacted the Wagner Act (1935) and, subsequently, the Taft-Hartley Act (1947). The impact on management of such expansionary uses of the statutory powers of the Board is obvious. Some of them are more apparent to the economist's eye, perhaps, than to the lawyer's. For example, the Board's mandatory bargaining policies had the effect of creating a special set of "rights" for unionized employees (and for them only), thereby imposing on the closing of unionized plants restrictions which were not applicable to *non*unionized plants. The competitive advantage thus conferred on the nonunionized employer is obvious, as is the corresponding disadvantage to the unionized employer. Economic decision making for the *unionized* employer, therefore, has a dimension which does not confront his nonunionized competitor, and (as we have seen and shall see further) the law which governs that dimension has been characterized by uncertainty, thus further handicapping the unionized employer.

The controversy over decision bargaining has been going on for more than two decades, and (while, more recently, the law has been stabilized to some degree) there is still no real certitude for the unionized employer concerning the degree to which his duty to bargain (or what will, after the fact, be held by the Board to have been his duty to bargain) cuts across his ability to manage effectively. Although the thrust of Board doctrine in this area has been generally expansionary, the development of the law has been characterized by twists and turns which, even when they favor the employer (as has happened from time to time and is happening as we write[49]), serve nonetheless to create uncertainty and thus complicate the decision-making process. Moreover, as we have seen, the courts have not entirely agreed with the Board's views of the mandatory duty to bargain. This further enhances uncertainty, risks, and costs for the unionized employer. It goes without saying that most businessmen would prefer not to subject their decision-making process to the bargaining process. This disposition is likely the result not so much of antiunion animus as of a desire to be "unencumbered," to use a word which the Supreme Court will later use in this context. The unionized employer, therefore, must try to assess whether he has, in fact, a bargaining duty and, if so, how it is to be satisfied. Notify the union and bargain, on request, over the impending decision? Or only over its effects? If (as will very often be the case) bargaining would entail burdens on the decision-making process which are unacceptable and ought to be avoided, if the law permits—and if the law seems to be favorable on his fact situation—shall the employer assume the risk and proceed without bargaining, thus possibly incurring the cost of a Board proceeding (even though he ultimately prevails)? Shall he risk, on the other hand (if he does not prevail), a Board order nullifying his decision? Or shall he play it safe and bargain, even though there are business disadvantages and other costs involved in that course? And finally, even if he bargains to impasse and then proceeds unilaterally (as the Board has said he is permitted to do), he runs the risk that the Board will later decide that he did not, in fact, sufficiently discharge his obligations under the Act. That this is not mere theoretical speculation will be demonstrated in the Board's decisions in the *Los Angeles Marine* and *Milwaukee Spring* cases discussed in Chapter VI.

4. *The Hiatus in the Push for Workers' Rights Under the Act*

A few years after *Ozark Trailers* the complexion of the Board *changed* again with the appointments made by President Richard M. Nixon. Among other things, this brought to the chairmanship a seasoned labor lawyer, Edward B. Miller, of Chicago. The Board thereupon acquired that kind of practical acquaintance with day-to-day labor-management relations which had been so signally lacking during much of its existence, including especially the era which invented decision bargaining and produced the decisions in *Fibreboard II, Ozark Trailers,* and the other cases which we have been discussing.

At the same time having experienced, as a practitioner, the uncertainties resulting from shifting political winds at the Board over the years, Chairman Miller appeared loath to add further to such uncertainties for others. Accordingly, the Board during his term made no effort to reverse or eliminate the decision-bargaining doctrine. Instead (anticipating the balanced approach to workers' rights and management rights which the Supreme Court would adopt a decade later in the *First National Maintenance Corp.* case), the Miller Board took a more limited view of the mandatory decision-bargaining requirement. In doing so, it paid close attention to the *Fibreboard* opinions, especially the opinion of Justice Stewart. Two cases will serve to illustrate.

In *General Motors Corporation*,[50] the employer sold its Houston truck center to a company called Trucks of Texas. It did so without bargaining with the union (the United Automobile Workers) which represented certain of its employees. Trucks of Texas subleased from General Motors the premises occupied by the center, took title to all of its equipment, and became a franchised GM truck dealer. The NLRB hearing officer nevertheless found that the transaction was in fact a contracting out and that, under *Fibreboard*, General Motors had a duty, *which it failed to carry out,* to bargain over its decision.

The Board (with two holdover members dissenting[51]) rejected that reasoning, holding that the transaction had clearly been a genuine sale marked by a transfer of assets and "an arm's-length withdrawal of capital" by General Motors, while Trucks of Texas made "a corresponding investment." The Board noted that the courts had rejected attempts by earlier Board decisions to impose mandatory bargaining upon "elemental management decisions, such as plant closings and plant removals."[52] Although the Board had not previously dealt with the sale of a business, the Miller Board felt that the issue was controlled by the principle that

> decisions...in which a significant investment or withdrawal of capital will affect the scope and ultimate direction of an enterprise, are matters essentially financial and managerial in nature. They thus lie at the very core of entrepreneurial control and are not the types of subjects which Congress intended to encompass with "rates of pay, wages, hours of employment, or other conditions of employment."[53]

The Miller Board also anticipated the concept of "amenability" as a criterion for the imposition (or not) of mandatory decision bargaining,[54] saying that such entrepreneurial decisions "involve subject areas as to which the determinative financial and operational considerations are likely to be unfamiliar to the employees and their representatives."[55]

The Board concluded by holding that, even though it was not required to bargain over its decision, General Motors had an obligation to bargain over its effects, but (contrary to the hearing officer and Member John Fanning) the Board felt that it had met that obligation.

The other case arose less than a year later and involved the shutdown of Summit Tooling Company.[56] This case was not so simple and clear-cut as *General Motors*. It involved allegations that the discharge of several employees and, indeed, the shutdown itself were motivated by antiunion animus, rather than the economic reasons asserted by the employer, as well as allegations that Summit had failed to discharge its duty to bargain.

The hearing officer found Summit pretty much guilty as charged, and the remedy which he proposed would have required Summit to reopen. The Board[57] largely agreed with the trial hearing officer, but (except for Member Fanning) disagreed with his finding of a decision-bargaining obligation, as well as with his proposed reopening order.

On the first point, the panel majority held that what Summit did was clearly "a major change in the nature of [its] business" and to require decision bargaining would (echoing Chief Justice Warren in *Fibreboard*) "significantly abridge *Summit*'s freedom to manage its own affairs." The decision (echoing and citing the *Darlington* case) adds: "We do not believe that the Act contemplated eliminating the prerogative of an employer, as here, to eliminate itself as an employer."[58]

There being no obligation to bargain about the decision, the Board (except for Member Fanning, as we have noted) rejected the "drastic remedy" proposed by its hearing officer. It held, however, that Summit had failed in its duty to bargain over the *effects* of its shutdown decision, and the remedy for this violation included a rather elaborate scheme intended to "restore some measure of economic strength to the union" in the bargaining to come.[59]

As the *General Motors* and *Summit Tooling* cases illustrate, the Nixon-Ford years were relatively uneventful in terms of our interest here—the Act as a vehicle for the creation and implementation of a theory of a worker's right in his job. Indeed, the issue of decision bargaining itself did not figure at all in several cases in which, at other times in the Board's history, it would have played a pivotal part.[60]

Mr. Miller left the Board upon the expiration of his term late in 1974. He was succeeded by Mrs. Betty Murphy, appointed by President Gerald Ford in 1975. Like Miller, Mrs. Murphy had been a practicing labor lawyer, and her term was also marked by no dramatic developments in respect of decision bargaining or the right-in-the-job thesis advanced in *Ozark Trailers*. When Mrs. Murphy was replaced in 1977 by John Fanning as Chairman, however, the Board, as we shall see, went once again boldly on the offensive in terms of the worker's right in his job and, in two cases decided several years apart, it plunged far beyond *Ozark*.

Before looking at those cases, however, we must examine how the United States Supreme Court dealt with decision bargaining in the *First National Maintenance* case, the first case since *Fibreboard* in which the decision-bargaining concept was the central issue.

V. The *First National Maintenance* Case

1. *Introduction*

Up to this point, we have been observing the development of a theory of "rights-in-the-job" as a corollary to, or a product of, management's duty to bargain over shutdown decisions. We have been observing what we called the tussle between the Board and some of the federal courts of appeal over the nature and extent of that bargaining obligation. We have seen in *Darlington* that when the shutdown is total—turning the key and going out of business—the Act does not apply. Its antidiscrimination provisions cannot reach the employer who goes out of business totally because he cannot abide the idea of doing business with a union; but also its compulsory collective bargaining provisions cannot reach the employer who, innocent of any antiunion motive, chooses to go totally out of business without bargaining with his union over his decision to do so.

In the *First National Maintenance* case, for the first time, the Supreme Court addressed the employer's duty to bargain—and particularly the decision-bargaining obligation—*in a plant-closing context.* The closing was not *total,* as we shall see, but merely the shutdown of a single operation—the kind of situation which the Board calls a "partial closing" and which it felt to have been left untouched by the Court in *Darlington* insofar as the employer's obligation to bargain is concerned.

The *First National Maintenance* case deserves our close attention for several reasons. It is a case involving the duty to bargain with a union over a plant-closing decision. It is the first utterance of the Supreme Court on that issue, and it represents a major effort by the Court to provide a fairly definitive treatment of the nature of the employer's bargaining obligation and, especially, the *limits* of that obligation. And, finally, the Board's reaction to *First National Maintenance* provides a striking study of the relationship between the judiciary and an administrative agency —particularly the NLRB—which is resisting correction by the Court.

The case further merits study because it provides an indispensable foundation to the analysis of some subsequent cases, which, at the Board level, took a sharply differing path.

2. The Case

First National Maintenance Corporation (or FNM, as the Supreme Court opinion[1] referred to it) provided, in the New York area, personnel, equipment, and supplies necessary to perform maintenance and related services for commercial and institutional customers. One such customer, Greenpark Care Center, operated a nursing home.

A contract for services between FNM and Greenpark was made in April 1976 and was essentially a cost-plus arrangement. Greenpark agreed to reimburse FNM for its labor cost and, in addition, to pay FNM a fixed fee of $500 per week for the services performed. Greenpark was one of several such customers. FNM hired the personnel separately for each such operation, and never transferred personnel between customer locations.

The relationship between Greenpark and FNM was troubled almost from the start. In November 1976, barely six months into the contract, the fixed fee was reduced at the insistence of Greenpark from $500 per week to $250. Then, in March 1977, Greenpark gave FNM a thirty-day termination notice, specifying "lack of efficiency" as the reason. Termination pursuant to that notice, however, was not effectuated (the reason does not appear), and FNM continued to perform the services. On June 30, 1977, FNM asked that its fee be restored to the original $500 level and a week later notified Greenpark that it would terminate service August 1 unless the increase was forthcoming. It was not, and on July 6, FNM gave Greenpark a final notice of termination to be effective as of August 1. (The adequacy of the termination notice was not an issue in the case.)

Meanwhile, some months earlier, a union had begun an organizing campaign among FNM's thirty-five Greenpark employees. An NLRB election was held on March 31, in which a majority of the employees voted for the union, and it was certified by the Board as bargaining representative on May 11. The union took no action pursuant to the certification until July 12. The relationship between FNM and Greenpark meanwhile continued to deteriorate. On July 12, the union requested a bargaining meeting "when it will be convenient." FNM did not reply, and on July 28, following on its July 6 notice to Greenpark, FNM notified its Greenpark employees that they would be terminated three days later.

The union immediately requested a delay in the termination to allow time for bargaining. FNM replied that this was impossible, citing the cost of thereby incurring still another thirty-day notice requirement if the August 1 deadline were to be overrun. FNM added that the termination was "purely a matter of money, and final." The union tried to persuade Greenpark to waive the new thirty-day notice period or to hire FNM's Greenpark employees, but it was unsuccessful.

The termination went forward as scheduled and the union filed charges under section 8(a)(5) of the Act. (The issue of antiunion animus was not raised in the case, which proceeded on the basis of an economically motivated decision by FNM to cease doing business at Greenpark.) The Board adopted the findings and conclusions of the administrative law judge (ALJ) who heard the case that FNM had violated section 8(a)(5) by refusing to bargain over its *decision* to terminate the Greenpark contract and by failing to bargain over the *effects* of that decision upon FNM's Greenpark employees. The Board added a conclusion of its own: that FNM also committed a refusal to bargain by its failure to respond to the union's July 12 request for negotiations.[2] The administrative law judge's reasoning was broad:

> When an employer's work complement is represented by a union and he wishes to alter the hiring arrangements, be his reason lack of money or a mere desire to become richer, the law is no less clear that he must first talk to the union about it.[3]

The quoted excerpt from the decision of the administrative law judge (like language of the Board which we have noted earlier) describes the mandatory bargaining duty in soft terms—as a mere obligation to "talk to the union"—and his decision goes on to suggest that such talk might have resulted in either (a) a transfer of the terminated employees (ignoring FNM's practice of not transferring), or (b) an agreement by Greenpark to use the employees itself (ignoring—indeed, not even mentioning—the testimony concerning Greenpark's refusal of the union request that it do just that). A little later in his decision, the ALJ abandons his soft rhetoric and sternly and sweepingly describes the management decision as "an absolutely mandatory subject of collective bargaining."[4]

The ALJ recommended (and the Board adopted) an order to bargain over both the decision and its effects. He did not propose an order for the *resumption* of the discontinued operations, but he did recommend back pay from the date of termination of the employees until the date when the bargaining obligation, imposed by his order, would be discharged. The Board added a refinement of its own: an order that if the Greenpark operations were not resumed, the former FNM Greenpark employees were to be rehired by FNM at its other operations thereby replacing, if necessary, more recently hired employees of FNM.[5]

The Court of Appeals for the Second Circuit enforced the Board's order, but employed a different rationale. Rejecting what it called the Board's *"per se"* theory of a bargaining duty (i.e., "a duty to bargain *whenever* an employer closes part of its business," even for purely economic reasons—a rather sweeping statement), the Court of Appeals held that "the correct approach is to establish a *presumption*" that a duty to bargain exists.[6] That presumption could be rebutted by showing that the purpose of the statute would not be furthered by such bargaining (for example, where bargaining would be futile or where there were "emergency financial circumstances").[7]

The Supreme Court reversed the decision of the Court of Appeals. Justice Harry A. Blackmun wrote the opinion for the majority (Justices William J. Brennan and Thurgood Marshall dissented). Justice Blackmun remarked at the outset on the conflict in the cases of decision bargaining, observing that the Second Circuit appeared to be at odds with the decisions of other federal courts of appeals, some of which, he noted, had held that bargaining is not required over any management decision involving "a major commitment of capital investment" or a "basic operational change,"[8] while others had held that there is no bargaining duty unless antiunion animus and a section 8(a)(3) violation are involved.[9] He also noted the inconsistency in some of the Board's own rulings and stated that the Supreme Court had agreed to review the case because of the "importance of the issue and the continuing disagreement between and among the Board and the Courts of Appeals."[10]

Clearly, the opinion was intended by the Court to clarify the state of the law, and clearly all the necessary elements were present: there was the issue of management's duty to bargain over (1) the decision to cease operations, and (2) the effects of that decision. There was also present the issue of the managerial interest in freedom in decision making as against the interest of the employees in their jobs (job rights), thus posing the critical question as to the extent to which Congress intended to abridge the former interest to serve the latter. Whether or not Justice Blackmun was altogether successful is less clear. Moreover, while the case may resolve the conflict among the *Courts of Appeals,* which was one of its objectives, the subsequent behavior of the *Board,* hereafter discussed, indicates that the Court's objective of settling the law *for the Board* as well was decidedly less successful than might have been expected.

Because of the importance of the decision, it will be useful to begin by summarizing what the Court held and then examining, in some detail, how the Court arrived at those conclusions.

First, like the Court of Appeals, the Supreme Court rejected the Board's *per se* rule for decision bargaining, which, as we have already noted, amounted in effect to a general rule that management decisions which will have an impact on jobs are, *by that fact,* subject to mandatory decision bargaining.

Second, the Supreme Court also rejected the lower court's presumption in favor of bargaining, which the Second Circuit had fashioned in lieu of the Board's *per se* rule.

Third, the Supreme Court fashioned its own criteria for determining whether a mandatory decision-bargaining obligation exists. Essentially, those criteria follow the line laid down by Justice Stewart in *Fibreboard,* distinguishing, in terms of their impact on the employment relationship, between management decisions which are clearly *not* subject to the bargaining duty and those which clearly are, and adding a third mixed category (into which *FNM* fell) consisting of situations in which, even though the management decision has a direct impact on employment, its purpose is "apart from the employment relationship" and its focus is on the business as such. For those cases, the Court devised a balancing test to determine whether or not the mandatory bargaining obligation should apply.

Fourth, in fashioning its balancing test, the Court displayed an awareness of some of the intensely practical problems (for both sides) involved in attempting to inject unions (and workers' rights) into the management decision-making process, and its intention appears to have been to arrest the Board's tendency to make employee rights and collective bargaining concerning them the primary and paramount consideration, while having little or no regard for the problems of the employer and the exigencies of his business situation.

Fifth, the Court's balancing test switches that emphasis for the cases in which it is to apply. Against the Act's objectives of promoting collective bargaining and protecting employees, it weighs the problems of running a business and the economic necessities which may confront an employer in a given situation. There is to be no *presumption* in favor of the mandatory duty to bargain; on the contrary, that duty is to be imposed upon the employer *only* when it can be shown that the benefits to labor-management relations *and* the collective bargaining process outweigh the burden that mandatory bargaining imposes on the conduct of the business. In short, the burden of proof, so to speak, is hereafter to

lie with those asserting the duty to bargain about the management decision, at least in those situations where the *business* motivation dominates
the *employment* aspect of a given managerial decision.

Sixth, there are indications that the Court, in its effort to clarify and
settle the law of decision bargaining, sought to lay down a rule of
broader application than was required by the case before it, although
some of the language used by the Court tends to cast a cloud on this
aspect of its ruling.

Turning now to the opinion itself and the manner in which the foregoing principles were developed, we find Justice Blackmun opening with a
crisp statement of the issue before the Court (and, in doing so, he clearly
poses the central issue of "decision bargaining"): "Must an employer
under its duty to bargain in good faith with respect to wages, hours and
other terms and conditions of employment...negotiate with the certified
representative of its employees over its decision to close a part of its
business?"[11]

Following his statement of the facts, Justice Blackmun reviews the
familiar history of the National Labor Relations Act and its objectives
with special reference to the duty to bargain. He then makes a series of
statements which, foreshadowing the line his opinion will take, reveals
his view that there are limits to the employer's bargaining obligation
under the Act: "Congress had no expectation that the elected union
representative would become an equal partner in the running of the
business enterprise in which the union's members are employed." He
adds: "Despite the deliberate open-endedness of the statutory language,
there is an undeniable limit to the subjects about which bargaining must
take place." And, quoting from a 1971 decision of the Court, he concludes: "In general terms, the limitation includes only issues that settle
an aspect of the relationship between the employer and the
employees."[12] Thus, Justice Blackmun makes it clear at the outset (as
Justice Stewart had done) that, the views of the NLRB notwithstanding,
there are limits to the extent to which the Act compels the employer to
admit the union to the managerial decision-making process.

Management decisions, as Justice Blackmun sees them, fall into three
classes, depending upon their primary thrust, and this, in turn, deter-
mines whether or not they are subject to the decision-bargaining obligation. First, there are those whose impact on the employment relationship
is only "indirect and attenuated" (advertising, finance, product design).
Justice Blackmun, with Justice Stewart, believes that such decisions are
clearly not to be subjected to mandatory bargaining. Second, and in contrast, are those decisions (e.g., concerning procedures on layoffs and

recalls to work) which, by their nature, are "almost exclusively 'an aspect of the [employment] relationship',"[13] and which, therefore, can appropriately be subjected to the mandatory bargaining process.

A third type of management decision, Justice Blackmun then notes, is the sort involved in this case which, although it had "a direct impact on employment, since jobs were inexorably eliminated by the termination," is nevertheless "wholly apart from the employment relationship," because the management decision "had as its focus only the economic profitability of the contract with Greenpark."[14] In other words, the decision is *primarily* a *business* one, forced and shaped by the economic realities facing the enterprise. As such, it is by no means obvious, as the Board would have it, that such a decision *must* be bargained over. On the contrary, Justice Blackmun thinks (as he says at another point) that there can be situations involving "economic necessity sufficiently compelling to obviate the duty to bargain,"[15] for "[m]anagement must be free from the constraints of the bargaining process to the extent essential for the running of a profitable business."[16] And Justice Blackmun clearly sees the management decision made by FNM in those fundamental terms, for he says: "This decision, involving a change in the scope and direction of the enterprise, is akin to the decision whether to be in business at all."[17] Indeed, FNM's decision was *precisely* a decision "whether to be in business at all," or any longer, at the Greenpark location.

Justice Blackmun recognizes the fact that so final a decision "touches on a matter of central and pressing concern to the union and its member employees"[18]—namely, continued employment. While not in any way rejecting or disparaging that concern or its legitimacy, Justice Blackmun makes clear in his ensuing discussion that, in his view, the existence of that concern does *not* (and in this he parts sharply from the Board's philosophy in *Ozark Trailers* and other cases) necessarily give rise to a mandatory duty to bargain over the management *decision*. At the same time, FNM's duty to bargain over the effects of the decision was noted by Justice Blackmun and had not been disputed by FNM.[19]

To put it another way—and in terms relevant to our search for concepts of workers' rights under the National Labor Relations Act—Justice Blackmun (and the Supreme Court majority for which he spoke) did not agree with the Board that there was to be found in the Act an *absolute* right of employees to participate through their union in management decision making; this right was to be triggered simply by the fact that a given decision could or would have impact on their jobs and that they were, in consequence, concerned. The Court, it made clear in *FNM*, will require more than that to give rise to a *right* (by way of NLRB mandate) to participate through collective bargaining *in the decision-making process.*

At the same time, Justice Blackmun had no problem in finding in the FNM situation a somewhat lesser right which comes into existence in nearly every plant-closing case (and most other situations involving decision bargaining): the right of the union to bargain over effects, that is, to be heard concerning the *impact* of the management decision on the affected employees and the right to engage in collective bargaining with a view toward avoiding or diminishing or cushioning that impact. This is no negligible right and, as we shall be seeing, Justice Blackmun thinks that in many situations it (rather than mandatory decision bargaining) holds the solution to the problems of workers and unions in plant-closing situations and to the policy judgment that they have a right to be heard. Meanwhile, observe how Justice Blackmun works his way toward a resolution of the conflict which the Board has consistently ignored: the conflict between the legitimate interests and concerns, in a plant-closing situation, of employees and unions on the one hand, and those of management on the other.

The resolution of that conflict, Justice Blackmun says, requires the Court to determine whether or not "the decision itself" is part of what he calls FNM's "retained freedom" to manage that part of its affairs which is "unrelated to employment."[20] Justice Blackmun here begins a careful definition of the limits, as he perceives them, to the Act's intrusion upon management's inherent right and duty to manage. Clearly, the Congress never intended to compel bargaining over affairs "unrelated to employment." Management's freedom to operate in those areas is unabridged by the Act; it is, to use Justice Blackmun's word, "retained." Moreover, the purposes of mandatory bargaining can only be served if the subject of the bargaining is "amenable to resolution through the bargaining process."[21] Presumably, by way of suggesting the kinds of things which may *not* be "amenable," Justice Blackmun notes (in language we have already referred to) that management needs to be "free from the constraints of the bargaining process" in respect of those matters "essential to the running of a profitable business." Since Congress has not explicitly defined those matters, Justice Blackmun provides a criterion. Significantly, he poses it in terms of the "employer's need for unencumbered decisionmaking" and, even more significantly, he specifies that it will apply even to those decisions which may have "a substantial impact on the continued availability of employment." His language follows:

[I]n view of an employer's need for unencumbered decisionmaking, bargaining over management decisions that have a substantial impact on the continued availability of employment should be required only if the benefit, for labor-management relations and the collective bargaining process, outweighs the burden placed on the conduct of the business.[22]

Thus Justice Blackmun fashions a balancing test of his own. The test is a fairly stringent one, for it would compel bargaining *only* when the benefits of bargaining outweigh its burdens. Justice Blackmun will go on to find the balance in this case to be *against* imposing a mandatory duty to bargain over the decision to discontinue the Greenpark operation (which he describes as "an economically motivated decision to shut down part of a business"[23]) but not without first engaging in an extensive survey of the respective interests and concerns of labor and management in decision-bargaining situations generally, and in this one in particular. In the course of that survey, he explicitly treats the problems and the goals of *both* parties—something the *Board* rarely does. With respect to a union's objectives, he says:

The union's practical purpose in participating [in decision-bargaining] will be largely uniform: it will seek to delay or halt the closing. No doubt it will be impelled, in seeking these ends, to offer concessions, information, and alternatives that might be helpful to management or forestall or prevent the termination of jobs.[24]

Mandatory bargaining over decisions, he observes at another point, "could afford a union a powerful tool for achieving delay, a power that might be used to thwart management's intentions in a manner unrelated to any feasible solution the union might propose."[25] This observation is made not out of a lack of sympathy with the aims and objectives of the union, but by way of emphasizing the unworkability—the perversity, in some cases—of compelling *mandatory* bargaining. It is useful here to return to that part of the opinion, from which we just quoted, in which Justice Blackmun describes the objectives and tactics of a union in a decision-bargaining situation. He went on thereafter to observe:

It is unlikely, however, that requiring bargaining over the decision itself will augment this flow of information and suggestions from the union. There is no dispute [however] that the union must be given a significant opportunity to bargain about these matters of job security as part of the "effects" bargaining mandated by Section 8(a)(5).[26]

Justice Blackmun here makes a sophisticated (and often overlooked)
point: Much of what unions legitimately seek to accomplish in decision
bargaining can as well be accomplished in the course of the "effects
bargaining" which is incumbent upon the employer in nearly all situations wherein any bargaining at all is required, but which does not
obstruct the essential decision-making function.

It is worth digressing for a moment to comment on another observation of Justice Blackmun's at this point. He remarks, almost as an aside,
that unions can seek limitations on plant closings in contract negotiations, but that this seems not often to be done.[27] We suggest an explana-
tion for this: The failure of unions to pursue the negotiating course (i.e.,
to make an effort to obtain in contract negotiations language which will
give them rights in shutdown situations possibly arising during the term
of the contract) is due, in many cases, to their anticipation of management resistance to any such limitation on necessary managerial flexibility. It is also due to the union's unwillingness to pay the cost, in
negotiating terms, of obtaining such limitations. Moreover, unions may
assume (not unreasonably, we suggest, given the tenor of many of the
Board decisions which are examined in this study) that the Board can be
counted on to impose such limitations, and this would be without cost to
the union or its members. Of course, management, too, can pursue an
advance solution of possible problems by obtaining from the union a
waiver of any rights the law may give the union to bargain over shutdown
decisions, and this is frequently done by way of the so-called management's rights clause of which we shall have more to say a little later.

We return to Justice Blackmun's opinion at the point where, having
treated the needs and objectives of unions, he displays an equal percep-
tiveness concerning management's objectives (the possibility of obtaining concessions) and problems (the possible need for speedy action,
secrecy, and flexibility, as well as the economics of taxes and finance).
He notes (without specific reference to FNM) that "[t]he employer also
may have no feasible alternative to the closing, and even good-faith
bargaining over it may be both futile and cause the employer additional
loss."[28]

Before applying his burden-benefits test to the task of balancing these
conflicting interests, Justice Blackmun makes a lengthy observation—
again, a point often overlooked—concerning the risks, especially for the
employer, in decision bargaining: The decisions as to whether to bargain
or not and, if so, how long and in what manner are all subject to being
later second-guessed by the Board, with costs which can be significant if
the Board disagrees with the employer's judgment concerning its
bargaining duty in the circumstances.[29]

Weighing all of the considerations he has enumerated (of which we have attempted to highlight only the most significant or illustrative), Justice Blackmun finds: "We conclude that the harm likely to be done to an employer's need to operate freely in deciding whether to shut down part of its business purely for economic reasons outweighs the incremental benefit that might be gained through the union's participation in making the decision." And, therefore, Justice Blackmun says: "[W]e hold that the decision itself is *not* part of Section 8(d)'s 'terms and conditions' over which Congress has mandated bargaining."[30]

Thus, Justice Blackmun, evaluating the facts against the burden-versus-benefits test which he earlier fashioned, decides that the Act does not require mandatory decision bargaining in a case like this one. It also seems clear in the statements quoted above that Justice Blackmun was not just addressing the case before him but was, at the same time, suggesting a broader application of the principles which he was enunciating. Note, for example, the use of the indefinite article ("an" employer) which suggests that the Court is laying down a general rule for cases involving a "shut down [of] part of [a] business for economic reasons"; and that rule is that in *any* such (economic shutdown) case no decision bargaining will be required, because "the harm likely to be done... outweighs the incremental benefit" which decision bargaining might have brought. The Court reinforces (if we read it correctly) this general holding by going on to declare that, in such economic shutdown cases, the management decision is not subject to mandatory bargaining, because it is simply not part of the "terms and conditions" of employment, as that phrase is used in section 8(d), over which bargaining is required.[31]

Perhaps some will see the foregoing as an over-interpretation of the majority opinion in *FNM,* but we believe that it is a plausible one given the kind of language which Justice Blackmun chose to employ. If our interpretation is correct, then *FNM* went further than many observers thought it did at the time, and certainly it went further than the Board, as we shall see, was prepared to accept. In any event, the result reached in *FNM* by the application of the Court's balancing test would seem sound and sensible given the circumstances of that case.[32]

Having done his best to enunciate principles and considerations which he deemed useful for the resolution of cases involving the controversial decision-bargaining doctrine, and having applied them to the case at hand to decide that it was not one in which mandatory decision bargaining should be required, Justice Blackmun concludes with a paragraph

designed, as he says, "to illustrate the limits of our holding."[33] To that
end, he enumerates some of the facts in *FNM* which influenced the
Court:

> (1) The discharged employees were not to be replaced. (This
> distinguishes the case from the *Fibreboard* situation.)
>
> (2) There was no "move" involved. (It was a plant shutdown, rather
> than a plant-removal situation, and hence no "runaway shop" issue can
> be posed.)
>
> (3) FNM sought only to reduce its economic loss.
>
> (4) There was no claim of "antiunion animus."
>
> (5) The union could not contribute to a resolution of the dispute be-
> tween Greenpark and FNM over the management fee.

Moreover, the Court notes, the union was not certified until well after
the FNM-Greenpark problems arose, and hence there was no "abroga-
tion of ongoing negotiations [with the union] or an existing bargaining
agreement."[34]

The opinion ends with language which appears to be addressed to
arguments based on the significance of capital investment as a factor in
determining the existence of a mandatory decision-bargaining duty.
Perhaps the Board or the union stressed, in argument, the *absence* of a
capital investment problem and urged that this justified the imposition of
mandatory bargaining. In any case, Justice Blackmun says that it is not
crucial for the element of capital investment to be present in order to
hold that decision bargaining is inappropriate. What he evidently saw as
an equivalent factor in this case provides the concluding note in his opinion:

> The decision to halt work at this specific location represented a signifi-
> cant change in petitioner's operations, a change not unlike opening a
> new line of business or going out of business entirely.[35]

A change in operations, in other words, like an investment decision, was
for FNM essentially a *business*—not an employment—decision. Mandatory bargaining over such decisions, the Court holds, is not required
by the Act.

3. *Summary of the Supreme Court Cases*

We pause, at this point, to take stock of how the Supreme Court has dealt with the issue of decision bargaining (and hence workers' rights) in the three decisions we have examined. In *First National Maintenance,* Justice Blackmun pursued his objective of producing an opinion which would clarify and settle the law with respect to mandatory bargaining over management decisions (including, particularly, those which might have an impact on employment) by laying down a set of rules or criteria as follows:

(1) If the impact on employment is merely "indirect and attenuated," no bargaining of any kind is required: such decisions are beyond the reach of the Act.

(2) Where that impact is direct—where the focus of the decision is primarily, and virtually exclusively, some aspect of the employer-employee relationship—bargaining over the decision is required. In other words, such a case is embraced by the statutory requirement to bargain over wages, hours, and other terms and conditions of employment.

(3) Where, although the impact on employment is direct, the *primary* purpose and thrust—the *focus*—of the management decision is the profitable operation of the business, decision bargaining is to be required *only* if its benefits outweigh its burdens ("only if the benefit for labor-management relations and the collective bargaining process outweighs the burden placed on the conduct of the business").[36]

Applying those criteria to the case at hand, the Court held that the decision by FNM to shut down one of its several operations (a "partial closure") was not subject to mandatory bargaining. Indeed, in the circumstances of the case, the Court ruled, "the decision itself is *not* part of Section 8(d)'s 'terms and conditions'...over which Congress has mandated bargaining."

We return to this aspect of the *FNM* decision in order to point up an aspect of the Court's approach in this and other cases which, we think, has been insufficiently noted. Although, as we have seen, the NLRB has consistently urged a rather transcendental view of the Act in general and its bargaining provisions in particular—that is, that property rights of employers (including the right to make business decisions) are subordinated to the Act's objectives regarding employees and their rights—the Court has just as consistently rejected this view, not only in *First National Maintenance,* but also earlier in *Fibreboard* and *Darlington.*

It is impossible, we think, to read Justice Blackmun's opinion without perceiving that he is quite uncomfortable with the active role which the

Board would give collective bargaining in the managerial decision-making process. He believes that businessmen need and ought to be "unencumbered" in the management of their business affairs, and that the Congress never intended that the union "would become an equal partner in the running of the business enterprise." Hence, in cases which fall into the third category of management decisions listed above (business-motivated decisions with impact on jobs), mandatory decision bargaining is not only *not* to be the norm, but it is not to be required in any case, unless it can be shown that its benefits outweigh the burdens which it imposes. With the balancing test thus formulated, it is no surprise (especially on the facts in *First National Maintenance*) that the Court found no case for the imposition of mandatory decision bargaining. Indeed, given the formulation, it would seem that the situation that would be resolved *in favor of* decision bargaining would be the exception, rather than the rule. It is perhaps with that in mind that the Court stated the outcome of the balancing in general—rather than specific—terminology ("an employer," rather than "this employer"): "We conclude that the harm likely to be done to an employer's need to operate freely in deciding whether to shut down part of its business purely for economic reasons outweighs the incremental benefit that might be gained through the union's participation in making the decision."

Thus the Court appears to provide a fairly clear indication as to how the balancing should come out in future cases of this kind (i.e., cases involving "an economically motivated decision to shut down part of a business"—in short, the typical "partial closing" case). Even though there is "a substantial impact on the continued availability of employment," the business aspect which is the "focus" of the decision is simply not one of the "terms and conditions" to which mandatory bargaining applies.

Both the concern for basic managerial freedom and the conviction that the Act was not intended to intrude upon it in cases of this type are threads which run through all three of the relevant Supreme Court decisions and not only give them coherence on this issue, but also define limits beyond which the Act does not and may not extend.

Thus, in *Darlington,* the Court was visibly dismayed by the boldness of what it termed "a proposition that a single businessman cannot choose to go out of business if he wants to." It asserted in response: "We hold that so far as the Labor Act is concerned, an employer has the absolute right to terminate his entire business for any reason he pleases."

It is significant that the Court, in affirming that the employer's right was "absolute," did so "so far as the Labor Act is concerned." The

Court did not say "so far as section 8(a)(3) is concerned," although that was what was chiefly involved in the case before it. It said that "the Labor Act"—all of it—had no application in the case of a total shutdown, and this holding, it would seem, applies no less to the duty to bargain than it does to the duty not to engage in antiunion activity. Indeed, no one (not even the Board) has seriously argued, since *Darlington,* that there can be a duty to bargain over a *total* shutdown (i.e., a going-out-of-business) decision.

Is there any reason why the logic of *Darlington* in respect of the *total* shutdown of a business should not apply equally to the total shutdown of a single plant (still assuming no purpose to chill unionism or other unfair labor practice which calls the Act into play)? None is apparent, and logic recommends it, as does property right theory. If there is a proprietary right which—even given the antiunion animus which admittedly existed in *Darlington*—was nevertheless "absolute," as against the Act, is it not plausible to reason that the same principle applies, *in the absence of animus,* when the same proprietary right is exercised less than totally?

There is strong evidence in the language of Justice Blackmun that he thought so, and we have already noted that the Eighth Court of Appeals and former Board Member Zagoria took that view.[37] Justice Blackmun's reference to FNM's "retained freedom to manage its affairs," as we noted earlier, is a recognition that there are proprietary rights which are not extinguished or abridged by the Act. *Darlington* recognizes that, and the outcome in *First National Maintenance* was in accord with the logic of *Darlington.* True, the issue and the argument had grown more complex and sophisticated in the sixteen years between *Darlington* and *First National Maintenance,* and Justice Blackmun apparently was persuaded that the question of decision bargaining ought at least to be given consideration. But it was clear from the outset of his opinion that he was not hospitable to the idea of such bargaining in the circumstances of that case. He suggested that effects bargaining might serve the purpose, without having an adverse impact on proprietary rights, and the balancing test which he devised was weighted, as we have noted, against decision bargaining.

We find the same concern for fundamental entrepreneurial rights in *Fibreboard*—the first case in the line—and not just in the concurring opinion of Justice Stewart. The Chief Justice, writing for the majority, meticulously noted that the Court's ruling "would not significantly abridge [the employer's] freedom to manage the business," leaving the strong implication that *if* the decision-bargaining duty *were* to have had that effect, the Court's decision might have been different. As to Justice

Stewart, we need not repeat here his views concerning the immunity of those decisions which "lie at the core of entrepreneurial control." Like Justice Blackmun, Justice Stewart found such decisions to be "excluded" from the "area subject to the duty of collective bargaining."

We have extended this summary beyond the *First National Maintenance* case because we feel it important to show a nexus—in terms of a concern for traditional proprietary (i.e., management) rights— between the three leading Supreme Court cases dealing, in one way or another, with plant closing and decision bargaining. The decisions seem to follow a path, better marked than some had thought, to the decision in *First National Maintenance,* and thus they are helpful in predicting where the Court will come out on the next decision-bargaining case (very likely one involving partial closing) which reaches it.

Meanwhile, there are clear indications in these cases that the Court is sensitive to the imperatives of running a business and is loath to impose upon business the extraordinary duty of bargaining with a union over critical management decisions. That this concern extends to single plant closings is not only inferable from the Court's language in the three cases we have been reviewing, it is *demonstrated* in the only such case that has come before the Court to date. In *First National Maintenance* (a decision which, as we are about to see, was highly unpopular with the Board), we saw the Court come down firmly against mandatory bargaining concerning the management decision in that case.

The next several years following *First National Maintenance* were, in some respects, about as controversial as any in the stormy history of the National Labor Relations Board. President Reagan had already taken office when the opinion in *First National Maintenance* was handed down. The Board, however, was still composed of appointees of previous administrations, including President Jimmy Carter's, and its general counsel, who figures largely in the next stage of our narrative, was himself a Carter appointee.

Faced with the ineluctable fact that, in due course, President Reagan would have the opportunity to alter the philosophy of the Board by appointments as members' terms expired, the Board and its general counsel—particularly the latter—spent the next couple of years building a body of case law which incorporated their convictions concerning workers' rights in plant shutdown situations. Working against time as they were, they appeared determined to get as much law on the books as possible before sitting members' terms expired and the Board's complexion changed. The sitting Board, of course, had every reason to suppose that President Reagan's appointees would be unlikely to be sympathetic with their interpretations and assumptions concerning the rights of employees and the rights of management under the Act. That, as we shall see, turned out to be very much the case.

First, though, the sitting Board had to deal with *First National Maintenance* and with the refusal of the Supreme Court in that case to accept the Board's rationale concerning the scope of the employer's duty to bargain, in general, and, in particular, the application of decision-bargaining theory in a plant-closing situation.

As we remarked earlier, the way in which *First National Maintenance* was received and dealt with by the Board provides an interesting case study in regulatory behavior. Moreover, even though the complexion of the Board has changed, the reactions of that Board and its general counsel to the Supreme Court's decision in *First National Maintenance* are a significant part of the history we are tracing. Those reactions reflect a point of view regarding the tension between workers' rights and management rights that, although absent from the present Board, could reassert itself readily with still another change in the makeup of this highly sensitive agency.

4. *The Board's Response to* First National Maintenance:
   The Lubbers "Guidelines"

Understandably, most students of labor law considered the decision in *First National Maintenance* a setback for the Board's decision-bargaining doctrine, particularly as applied to plant closings,[38] and William Lubbers, who served as the Board's general counsel from 1980 to 1984, soon set about trying to contain the damage.[39] In November 1981, Mr. Lubbers issued to the Board's field offices a memorandum entitled "Guidelines for Cases Arising under *First National Maintenance Corporation,*" which stated that it was to be "used as a guide for the investigation and administrative disposition of all pending and future cases that deal with this issue."[40]

In order to understand the significance of the "Guidelines," it is necessary to understand the role of the general counsel in the organization and operation of the National Labor Relations Board. He is the key figure in the Board's prosecutorial function; he controls the regional offices which receive and investigate charges, issue complaints, and schedule hearings. When in doubt about the law or the Board's position—when in doubt, for example, as to whether or not to issue a refusal-to-bargain complaint against an employer in a plant-closing situation—the field consults the general counsel. He formulates policy concerning the stance which the Board's enforcement arm will adopt on controversial legal issues, what new theories the Board will advance, and what interpretations of the Act it will adopt, advance, or alter. In addition, the general counsel is the instrumentality through which the Board exercises its extraordinary power, under section 10(j) of the Act, to apply for a court injunction in those cases in which it seeks to put a stop to alleged unfair labor practices, *even before a hearing is held on the charges.* Thus, in a case in which he believes that a plant closing, or other similar management action, is one over which the employer should engage in decision bargaining, the general counsel, in collaboration with the Board, is in a position to try to get that action halted by court order—to freeze the *status quo,* so to speak, and block management action—unless and until management bargains over its decision or it is determined that there is no obligation to bargain in that case.[41] In sum, the general counsel is a powerful and an influential official of the Board and not least in the areas of the interpretations to be given to the Act and to court decisions concerning it.

Despite their significance—especially at the time—we do not propose to analyze the Lubbers "Guidelines" in detail. Mr. Lubbers is no longer in office and his interpretations of the Act and of the cases are no longer authoritative. In addition, much of the doctrine for which he stood has already been repudiated by the present Board—at least in the area with which this study is concerned. At the same time, however, it cannot be denied that the Lubbers era with the Board is an important part of the history we are tracing. In addition to his "Guidelines," Mr. Lubbers later issued a report to the Board which we shall be discussing and which was almost certainly the most frontal attack on traditional management rights doctrine in the history of the Board. The views and the vocabulary adopted by Mr. Lubbers in that report and in his *FNM* "Guidelines" are essential to a proper understanding of the remainder of our case discussion, because they resonate not only in the decisions of the Board which agreed with Mr. Lubbers, but also in the revisionist decisions of its successor, which did not. The story of the Lubbers era is also an indispensable part of our history of the development of a theory of workers' rights under the National Labor Relations Act, for it constitutes something of a high-water mark in terms of Board doctrine concerning job rights in plant closings. At the same time, it helps to illustrate (along with the remainder of the cases which we shall be considering) the extreme swings in doctrine to which the NLRB is unfortunately prone, and the costs—in terms of uncertainty for litigants before the Board and instability in the law—that result from such swings.

In general, what Mr. Lubbers set out to do in his "Guidelines" was to minimize the impact of *First National Maintenance*. He did this by interpreting very narrowly its holding (limiting decision bargaining), thereby leaving still open a wide field for the operation of the Board's decision-bargaining doctrine. He was particularly concerned with leaving untouched by *FNM* the case of the single plant (or "partial") closing (one plant out of several), and the "Guidelines" go about that task this way: taking Justice Blackmun's almost casual remark that the decision confronting FNM was "akin to the decision whether to be in business at all," the Lubbers memorandum holds that *First National Maintenance* was, in fact, a going-out-of-business case, rather than merely a plant-closing or partial closing case. The relevant language of the Lubbers memorandum reads as follows: "The issue in *First National Maintenance* was whether a decision to go partially out of business is a mandatory subject, not whether a decision to close a plant is a mandatory subject."[42] On the facts of *First National Maintenance,* this interpretation seems to be dubious. What was done by FNM seems clearly to be more analogous to shutting down one plant of a multiplant operation than to deciding "to go partially out of business."[43] In ordinary usage, "to go partially out of business" suggests *ceasing* the manufacture of some type of product or the discontinuation of some type of service theretofore provided, and that is precisely what FNM did *not* do. It remained in the same business and continued to do the same things, in all respects, at its other locations.

At another point in his "Guidelines," Mr. Lubbers says, in effect, that *FNM* was *not* a case in which "the employer *intends to remain in the same business,* albeit elsewhere."[44] On the contrary, however, the quoted phrase describes *exactly* what FNM did. These things would hardly be worth noting, save for the interesting evidence they provide that General Counsel Lubbers had taken on a tough task and he knew it, and he was bound to have to strain a little to accomplish it. His efforts, however, hardly earned him widespread commendation from practitioners and litigants before the Board, plagued by new uncertainty where they had thought *FNM* had brought certainty. One such—a prominent management lawyer—called the "Guidelines" a "troublesome and regressive" effort to negate the broad application which the principles of *FNM* were intended to have.[45]

Not surprisingly, given his objective of minimizing the impact of *FNM,* Mr. Lubbers availed himself of the puzzling footnote 22 in *First National Maintenance* ("we of course intimate no view as to other types of managerial decisions") to argue that *FNM* provides *no guidance at all* in the several types of situation (including plant relocation and sale of business) listed by the Court as examples. It will be recalled that we reached a quite different conclusion concerning that much-discussed footnote.[46]

Two further aspects of Mr. Lubbers dogged exegesis of *FNM* must be noted before we take leave of it, for they will be reflected in later cases. Addressing himself to the Court's balancing test[47] (which, interestingly, he carefully reframes[48]), Mr. Lubbers describes "labor costs" (meaning wages and other costs imposed by union contracts) as being especially "amenable" to the bargaining process. From this it would follow that when the management decision turned on "labor costs," it would be subjected to mandatory bargaining. The effect of this "Lubbers doctrine," as we shall see, was to give labor costs a special status as an economic factor—actually a sort of immunity—and thus to safeguard unions from the adverse economic effects of bargaining which, because too successful for them, had become too costly for the employer.

The second aspect is Mr. Lubbers's repeated assurances to the Board staff that prior Board law remained essentially unaffected by the Supreme Court's decision in *First National Maintenance*—a point of view almost impossible to square with the language of the Court in that case. A completely different view was taken by former General Counsel Irving who thought that *First National Maintenance* "reflects...a general rule that decision bargaining is not required where the scope and direction of the enterprise is at issue." More specifically, the case held, Mr. Irving said, "that employers have no duty to bargain about partial closings."[49] While Mr. Irving's interpretation might be a shade too sweeping given the language of the Court, we think that, on the whole, it comes a great deal closer to an accurate statement of what the Court held than Mr. Lubbers did. As we shall see, Mr. Lubbers accomplished his purpose. His philosophy with respect to *First National Maintenance*, and with respect to plant-closing law generally, was fully embraced by the Board in its controversial *Milwaukee Spring* decision, with which we deal in the next chapter.

VI. A New Look in Workers' Rights: Bargaining Is Not Enough

1. *Introduction*

During the administration of President Carter, the Board once again underwent substantial change. The chairmanship passed from Betty Murphy to John Fanning, a twenty-year veteran on the Board and, as already noted, the man who invented decision bargaining. Fanning was widely respected for the high quality of his legal scholarship, his dedication to the job, and his prodigious industry. However, his entire career had been spent in government, more than half of it as a member of the National Labor Relations Board. In consequence, he lacked experience in the day-to-day practice of labor relations and any acquaintance with the fundamental problems of running a business. Nevertheless, Fanning's influence with his colleagues, even before he assumed the chairmanship, was enormous, and his philosophy is reflected in those Board decisions (of which we are about to see two further examples) that display a sort of transcendental view of the importance and efficacy of collective bargaining and of the status and legal effect of the union contract. In those cases, the Board was to hold squarely and for the first time something which had previously been only an inexplicit undertone in its decisions: a union contract *attaches* to the work performed by the employees covered by the contract, so that even in the absence of explicit restrictive language the work may not be moved to another location to be performed by other employees, no matter how uneconomical the operation covered by the union contract has become. To reach this objective, the Board, as we shall see, had to employ some imaginative statutory interpretation. It also had to disregard traditional concepts of management rights and the meaning of standard union contract clauses.

For reasons which we have just indicated, these things presented no problem to John Fanning as the Board entered an era—roughly extending over a five-year period, between 1978 and 1983—when it was to go further than ever before in the direction of establishing a right in the job for union members covered by a union contract.

We have noted that the "runaway shop" doctrine bars the removal of operations from one location to another when the move is motivated by antiunion animus. We have also examined the cases in which an employer contemplating a shutdown or a removal is required, before acting, to bargain over his decision and to bargain over its effects. But what about a case where there is no antiunion animus and where the employer has fully discharged his bargaining obligation as laid down by the Board—and then (proceeding, as the Board said he might, to implement his decision) he moves his work to another location where his labor costs will be more tolerable? The idea that the workers and their contract could thus simply be left behind was no doubt deeply troubling to workers' rights proponents at the Board. What good, some must have asked, to protect the right to join a union and to promote the negotiation of union agreements if the union agreement can be nullified before it has run its term? Is not this (except for the animus) almost as bad as the "runaway shop"? And does it not, therefore, call for a similar remedy?

On the other hand, management traditionally has had the right (unless it waives it in the union contract) to decide where its work will be performed and by whom. This conflict between "workers' rights," as that concept was developing at the Board, and the traditional concept of management rights was resolved by the Carter Board (more accurately, perhaps, the Fanning Board) in one of its most controversial decisions, the *Milwaukee Spring* case handed down in 1982. In that decision, the Board took a quantum step toward the establishment of a genuine right-in-the-job, arising out of the union contract and the Board's interpretation of section 8(d) of the Act. Although the Board's decision was subsequently overruled by the Reagan Board, its rationale is worth our attention for these reasons: it is an integral part of our historical narrative; it represents an unusually bold stroke on behalf of workers' rights; and the underlying thesis of the case could reappear in another era in the National Labor Relations Board's windswept history.

The ground for the *Milwaukee Spring* decision had partly been laid in the Lubbers "Guidelines" for the *First National Maintenance* case with Mr. Lubbers's instruction that "labor costs" were a special kind of economic factor. The way was further paved in the 1978 decision in the *Los Angeles Marine* case, *infra,* which added sinews to the idea that labor costs under a union contract are not easily escaped from, even when the conduct of the employer (in respect of his motive and the discharge of his bargaining obligations) has otherwise been blameless. Once again, for the sake of the narrative, we depart from a chronological treatment, and we deal with the *Milwaukee Spring* case first, because it is far and away the more important of the two cases.

2. Milwaukee Spring I

The *Milwaukee Spring* case,[1] first decided by the NLRB in the Fall of 1982, came a year after *First National Maintenance* and six months after the Lubbers memorandum. Aside from the fact that the Board itself clearly viewed it as a milestone case, *Milwaukee Spring I* is important for several reasons:

(1) It involved a "partial closing" by way of work removal (i.e., shifting work from one plant to another) and, before making the relocation decision, Milwaukee Spring discussed it with the union (a local of the United Automobile Workers) and sought to get the union to engage in so-called concession bargaining.[2] Discussions were held, but they proved fruitless, and the employer began implementing the decision to move.

(2) The union and the Board's general counsel formally acknowledged by stipulation that the employer did engage in decision bargaining and was willing to engage in effects bargaining. Nevertheless, the Board decided that Milwaukee Spring had violated the Act in that, when the move was finally made (after the bargaining impasse), it was made without the union's consent.

(3) In addition to finding a section 8(a)(5) bargaining violation, the Board held the employer guilty of violating section 8(a)(3) (discouragement of union activity—the *Darlington* issue), notwithstanding the fact that the Board's general counsel and the union both stipulated that there was no antiunion animus.

(4) Even though *Milwaukee Spring I* was reversed by the Reagan Board in *Milwaukee Spring II,* and that decision was affirmed by the federal appellate court, as we shall be discussing, that case (or one like it) may yet go to the Supreme Court and the Board's original position in *Milwaukee Spring* may yet find some vindication in whole or in part.

In any case, the reasoning of the Board in *Milwaukee Spring I* is so strongly supportive of the concept of a right-in-the-job that it merits our attention in this study on that ground alone (even if there were not the possibility that the philosophy of the Fanning Board may one day rise again).

Milwaukee Spring Division is one of four companies making up Illinois Coil Spring Company.[3] For some years, Milwaukee Spring had had contractual relations with the UAW local union. In January 1981, the company sought to engage in concession bargaining with the union, requesting that it forego a wage increase scheduled for April 1 and asking, in addition, for other improvements in the union contract, overtures which the union ultimately rejected.[4] On March 12, Milwaukee Spring informed the union that the economic situation was worse than it had originally estimated, owing, among other things, to the loss of a contract which meant $200,000 a month in revenue. The company proposed moving its assembly operations to another plant of the parent company. That plant was not unionized, and its hourly rates and fringe costs were substantially lower than called for by the UAW contract at Milwaukee Spring.[5] On March 22, the company informed the UAW that it was willing to bargain over alternatives to relocating its assembly operations, and it also advised the union that it needed relief if it was to avoid moving its molding operations as well. The next day the employer was told that the union membership had voted against "accepting $4.50 in wages and $1.35 in fringe benefits," but was willing to have discussion continue.

On March 29, Milwaukee Spring furnished the union with a memorandum of the terms upon which it would keep the assembly operations in Milwaukee. The union's representative went through that document with the employer and remarked that the proposals "came close to the lowest levels that it [the union] could accept," although he added that "this would not foreclose bargaining." Six days later, however, the employer was informed that the union membership "rejected consideration of labor contract concessions."[6]

The Board's decision stated (pursuant to the parties' stipulation) that the relocation thereafter undertaken by Milwaukee Spring was "due solely to the comparatively higher labor costs" under the UAW agreement and that the decision was "economically motivated and not the result of [anti]union animus." As had also been stipulated, the Board found that Milwaukee Spring "had bargained with the union over the decision to relocate the assembly operations" and "has been willing to engage in effects bargaining with the union."[7]

At the hearing, counsel for the union and for the Board's general counsel (Mr. Lubbers) contended that Milwaukee Spring had violated both section 8(a)(3) and section 8(a)(5) by the decision to make the move (a) *during the term* of the labor agreement without the union's consent, and (b) solely on the ground of the labor costs under that agreement. This position was based fundamentally on the Board's interpretation of the employer's bargaining duty as defined in section 8(d) of the Act.

Section 8(d) was added to the Act by the Taft-Hartley Act in 1947. It undertook to define the duty to bargain which the Act imposed on employers and (beginning in 1947) on unions. It thus implements section 8(a)(5), which we have been discussing, in respect of the employer's duty to bargain. Among other things, the Taft-Hartley Act aimed at more responsible behavior by unions and greater stability in labor-management relations, especially where the parties had entered into a contract. To that end, section 8(d) provided that where there was a union contract in force, "no party to such contract shall terminate or modify such contract" save upon following certain detailed procedures. In addition, section 8(d) says, neither party is required "to discuss or agree to any modification of the terms and conditions contained in a contract for a fixed period, if such modification is to become effective" before the contract, by its terms, would be open for such modification.

The theory developed by the resourceful Mr. Lubbers in *Milwaukee Spring* involved a novel use of section 8(d). The Board argued that the relocation of operations by Milwaukee Spring constituted a "modification of the terms and conditions" of the UAW contract within the meaning of section 8(d), and it pointed to the statutory language to the effect that the section "shall not be construed as requiring either party to discuss or agree to any modification" to take effect during the life of the contract.

Now the threshold question of statutory interpretation here is this: when an employer elects to relocate his operations, and he relocates them to a place where the existing union contract does not apply, is he thereby engaging in a "modification" of any "terms and conditions contained in" the union agreement, or is he merely rendering that agreement no longer operative when he ceases operations at the location to which the agreement applies? This question lies at the heart of the debate over the application of section 8(d) to a situation like the one in *Milwaukee Spring*. The inability of the Board to point to any specific "term" or "condition" of the UAW contract that Milwaukee Spring was "modifying" is a further issue, and one to which we shall return.[8]

There are, in addition, two other issues which we have not encountered before. It will be recalled that it was *stipulated* in the case that Milwaukee Spring had done all the bargaining required by the Act. So the first new question is this: are there circumstances under which engaging in decision bargaining (or being willing to do so) is not sufficient to protect an employer against the Board? The second question is: if the union refuses, when invited, to engage in decision bargaining—or if it does agree to bargain but refuses to concur in the management decision—is the employer nevertheless barred from going ahead unilaterally?

It will be recalled that early on when the Board was engaged in justifying its then new decision-bargaining doctrine, it laid great stress on the fact that the employer is not required to bargain *to agreement* and that, if agreement is not in fact possible (that is, when there is an impasse), he is free to move unilaterally.[9] An impression was thus created that an employer willing to provide the union with notice and an opportunity to engage in bargaining over his decision (and over its effects) could safely move ahead in the event that the union proved unable or unwilling to deliver any relief which solved the employer's problem. That turned out, rather shockingly, not to be the case, insofar as the Board which decided *Milwaukee Spring I* was concerned.

In *Milwaukee Spring,* the Fanning Board was faced with an employer who had attempted to behave as prescribed in earlier Board decisions (in which Mr. Fanning had played an influential part). Nevertheless, the Fanning Board now held that such an employer had violated the Act. The Board, relying heavily on section 8(d), held that the union was under no obligation to negotiate or to agree to a "modification" of the contract. Under those circumstances, the employer was prohibited, absent the consent of the union, from taking the action which it did. That action was, in the Board's view, an impermissible unilateral modification of the union agreement. As we observed earlier, the Board failed to point out just what part of the UAW contract was being modified. That is not surprising. There was no such provision. Indeed, as we shall see, there was language to the opposite effect.

Thus we come to a third issue: was section 8(d) really intended to apply to (and abridge seriously) the employer's rights, as such rights had theretofore been understood, in a decision-bargaining situation, and can the employer's move to a new location which is not barred by any language in the union contract really be a "modification" of that contract within the meaning of section 8(d)?

Milwaukee Spring I confronted us with a major qualification to the decision-bargaining doctrine. It was not sufficient, it now appeared,

that, faced with the need to close or move a plant, an employer be willing
to engage in decision bargaining. If he had a contract with a union which
had some time to run and the union refused to consent to his proposed
action, or even to discuss the matter, the employer, in the Fanning
Board's view, was nevertheless immobilized by section 8(d). The entrepreneurial imperatives which, as we noted earlier, have concerned the
Supreme Court in all three of the key decisions were pointedly ignored by
the Board. Under the Board's rule, the employer's only relief in this
situation lies in obtaining the consent of the union. That may take one or
the other of two forms: (1) the union agrees to engage in bargaining over
the move and, in the course of the bargaining, agrees to the move, or (2)
the union has earlier agreed in negotiations to contract language which
authorizes the employer to make the move without further consultation
with the union.

As we have seen, the union in *Milwaukee Spring* rejected (1). The company, citing language in the contract, argued (2). It based its position on
two different parts of the UAW agreement: the "recognition clause" and
the "management rights clause." Because of the relevance of provisions
of this sort to the issue of rights-in-the-job, they are worth our attention.

The recognition clause in the UAW contract provided that the union
was recognized for the "production and maintenance employees in the
company's plant in Milwaukee."[10] The purpose of the recognition clause
in any union contract is generally twofold: From the union's standpoint
it reaffirms, by agreement of the employer, the representative status of
the union. From the employer's standpoint it defines and limits the
bargaining unit and the operations or facility covered by the agreement.
The company's argument with respect to the recognition clause was
simply that its language confined the *application of the contract* to the
operations at Milwaukee. In consequence, when those operations moved
away from Milwaukee, the contract no longer had anything on which to
operate and thus, rather than being "modified" by the move, it simply
became inoperative. The Board in *Milwaukee Spring I,* however, rejected
this argument, stating that the contract language was merely a "descriptive recitation of the physical location of the facilities at the time of the
contract's negotiation" and it had no further effect. This holding appears to have been based on a misreading of an earlier case, as well as a
misunderstanding of the function of the recognition clause in a union
contract.[11]

The Board then turned to the issue of the contract's management
rights clause. Among other things, that clause provided that "the Company shall have the exclusive right to manage the plant and business and

direct the working forces." The management clause went on to specify some of the rights embraced within the foregoing general statement of the "exclusive" rights of management. They included the right "to plan, direct and control operations, determine the operations or services to be performed in or at the plant...to introduce new and improved methods, materials or facilities."[12] The issue was the extent to which the quoted language preserved management's flexibility and mobility. Milwaukee Spring argued, *inter alia,* that the clause, and particularly the phrase "determine the operations to be performed in or at the plant"—an "exclusive" right reserved by management in the contract—gave it the right to carry out, without union consent, the shift of operations from one location to another. The Board rejected this argument, stating that "we find nothing in this clause which *expressly* grants Respondent [Milwaukee Spring] the right to move, transfer, or change the location of part of its operations from its Milwaukee facility to another facility in order to avoid the comparatively higher labor costs imposed by the collective bargaining agreement containing the management-rights clause."[13]

There are three disturbing aspects to the foregoing holding of the Board, and since they go to the heart of the ongoing debate over the impact of the Act and the union agreement on the managerial decision-making function, they are unlikely to be put permanently to rest by a "new" Board—or any other. It serves the long-range objectives of this study, therefore, to examine them in some detail.

First, the Board is here adumbrating a theory, which its general counsel will more fully develop,[14] that once a union is in place management must bargain back its traditional rights to run the business. As more fully discussed below, it is our view (shared, incidentally, by the Reagan Board, as we shall see) that such a view not only is unsound as a matter of statutory interpretation, but it runs squarely against traditional views of what the Act intended to accomplish and what effect a union agreement has on preexisting rights of management.

Second, while the word "expressly" in the context of the rest of the sentence quoted above makes the Board's statement *literally* true, the holding bespeaks a lack of familiarity with the language of management rights clauses generally and with what professional labor relations practitioners understand and mean such language to accomplish. The management rights clause in the Milwaukee Spring contract is by no means unusual. Indeed (although not perfectly drafted), the clause is quite consonant with the terminology that labor relations draftsmen employ when management means to reserve to the maximum all of its traditional rights to run the business, except as they may have been "expressly limited" (as the agreement here said) by other provisions. It is difficult to understand how the Board could ignore the broad sweep of the language in general, and, in particular, how it could overlook the import of such phrases as "to manage the plant and business," to "direct and control operations," to "determine the operations...to be performed...at the plant," and "to change...facilities." However, the Board has traditionally had difficulty interpreting management rights clauses.[15]

Third, the use of the phrase "in order to avoid the comparatively higher [union] labor costs" provides a further strong—perhaps decisive —clue both to the Board's objective and to its erroneous interpretation of the management clause. As we shall be pointing out later, the Carter Board and its general counsel, Mr. Lubbers, were strongly of the view that management's right to decide where it shall engage in business is heavily abridged in any situation in which the Board perceives that a relocation decision was influenced by union-imposed labor costs.[16]

The Board went further. Based upon its above-described finding that by failing to comply with section 8(d) Milwaukee Spring violated section 8(a)(5), the Board went on to hold that the company was in violation of section 8(a)(3), *notwithstanding that it had been stipulated that there was no antiunion animus in the case.* In reaching this rather surprising conclusion, the Board in *Milwaukee Spring I* relied heavily on its decision about four years earlier in the *Los Angeles Marine* case. We discuss that case next. By way of summary, the reasoning on this point in *Milwaukee Spring I* ran this way: the midterm relocation was contrary to the provisions of section 8(d) and was "in derogation of [Milwaukee Spring's] bargaining obligation" under that section. For that reason, and because the purpose of the move was to obtain relief from the labor costs under the UAW agreement, the move was (quoting from *Los Angeles Marine*) "inherently destructive of employee interests" and, therefore, a violation of section 8(a)(3), as well as of section 8(a)(5).[17] Thus the Board managed to find an antiunion violation and a bargaining duty violation in the teeth of the *stipulation* by the parties that there was *no* antiunion animus and that the employer fully satisfied the requirements of both decision and effects bargaining! We believe that this apparent inconsistency can be explained by what we have earlier said concerning the Board's historical view of collective bargaining as a sort of transcendent value and preemptive congressional objective. Under that view, the union agreement, once arrived at, is entitled to and must be accorded a special and protected status, and this is what the Board sought to do in *Milwaukee Spring I.*

We conclude our review by remarking on the way that the Board in *Milwaukee Spring I* got around the *First National Maintenance* case.

It will be recalled that the Supreme Court had placed considerable emphasis on the need to give consideration to the employer's problems in running a business. How could the Board manage to square that prescription with the rather harsh treatment meted out in *Milwaukee Spring I* to an employer who, the Board admitted, had real economic problems and who had acted in good faith; who was guilty of no anti-union animus; and who had (or thought he had) discharged fully his bargaining obligation under the Act? The answer is that the Board (perhaps encouraged by General Counsel Lubbers's "Guidelines" memorandum downplaying *First National Maintenance*[18]) made no serious effort to do so. Instead, it contented itself with a footnote simply asserting that *First National Maintenance* "has no bearing on this case."[19]

The Board's remedy in *Milwaukee Spring I,* although not unprecedented for the Board, was nevertheless strong and imposed a heavy cost on the exercise of managerial judgment by an employer seeking to solve economic problems. The company was ordered to rescind the relocation decision, and (to the extent that the decision had already been implemented) to return the operations to Milwaukee, and to offer reinstatement with back pay to employees laid off in consequence of the removal decision.

The case went to the Seventh U.S. Court of Appeals on a petition by the company for review of the Board's order and a cross petition by the Board for enforcement of its order. Thereafter, the composition of the Board changed, in consequence of the appointments of President Reagan as the terms of the Carter Board members expired, and in August 1983, while the case was still pending and undecided in the Seventh Circuit Court of Appeals, that court granted a motion made by the "new" (Reagan) Board to remand the case to it to allow "further consideration" of its predecessor's decision.[20] The result was *Milwaukee Spring II,*[21] reversing the earlier decision and explicitly repudiating much of its rationale.[22]

The Reagan Board's decision provides (along with that Board's subsequent decisions in two other cases involving discontinuation of operations) an insight into current thinking at the Board concerning plant closings, decision bargaining, and the conflict between workers' rights and management rights. In order, however, to appreciate fully what *Milwaukee Spring II* held, it will be helpful—indeed, it is pretty much essential—to read what the "old" (Carter) Board had held in *Los*

Angeles Marine, the case that laid the groundwork for *Milwaukee Spring I,* and to read what the indefatigable Mr. Lubbers did with those two cases. As we shall see, *Los Angeles Marine* promoted the concept that the union contract, once made, is immutable and inescapable unless the union consents. Mr. Lubbers came out with a series of interpretations of the law, based in part on the two cases, which, had they prevailed, would have altered, permanently and drastically, traditional concepts of management rights and the legal effect of a union contract. Aside from its interest as history and as theater, Mr. Lubbers's last major exegetic exercise is also an almost indispensable guide to what the Reagan Board will be getting at in *Milwaukee Spring II.* The Board's decision in *Los Angeles Marine* was key to that exercise.

3. *The* Los Angeles Marine *Case*

Although one commentator later described *Los Angeles Marine* as "one of the greatest of the intrusions of the Board into the area of managerial discretion,"[23] the case nevertheless did not incite any special attention when it was handed down. It was not until four years later, when it seemed to have been suddenly "discovered" in *Milwaukee Spring I,* that *Los Angeles Marine* began to appear to have been something of a landmark.

The salient facts in this case were broadly similar to those in *Milwaukee Spring.* Los Angeles Marine Hardware Co., a wholesale distributor of marine hardware, had had a twenty-year bargaining history with the Teamsters' Union. Over time, the labor costs under the Teamster contact became increasingly burdensome and uncompetitive. The company's efforts to get the union to negotiate concessions were fruitless. Ultimately, after fully explaining the reasons for its action and seeking, still unsuccessfully, to reach an agreement with the union, the company removed operations to another location. The company even discussed the possibility of transferring employees *and* the Teamster contract to the new location provided it could obtain some relief from the wage costs under the existing contract. But the union was unresponsive, and, in due course, the move was made. New employees were hired at a lower wage, and the union responded with charges of unfair labor practices, based on the discrimination and the bargaining provisions of the Act.[24]

The decision of the administrative law judge before whom the case was tried was adopted, in its entirety, by the Board. Much of the twenty-page decision is taken up with the rather complex facts and with the resolution of conflicts in the testimony. Our concern is not so much with those details as with the principles laid down in this ground-breaking case. Certain facts about the case are, however, worthy of note. The decision seemed to go out of its way to set up a strong *economic* justification for what Los Angeles Marine did—and then boldly swept it aside, thus dramatizing the transcendence of the union contract over the economics of the enterprise. This view of the union contract lay at the core of the philosophy of the Carter Board (even before the advent of Mr. Lubbers) and was emphatically projected in this case and in the later decision in *Milwaukee Spring I,* which we have just discussed. Thus the Board in the *Los Angeles Marine* decision acknowledged that the company had "a legitimate adverse economic problem"; that the decision to move "was an economic one and not based upon unlawful considerations"; that the company had fully satisfied its bargaining obligations ("there can be no basis for finding that Respondents failed to satisfy their obligation to bargain about the decision and its effects"); and on the discrimination issue, that the evidence did not support the charge that Los Angeles Marine discouraged its employees from seeking employment at the new location or that it made the move to rid itself of the union.[25]

Despite these sweeping findings which, prior to the *Los Angeles Marine* case, might have exonerated the company from the unfair labor practice charges, the Board found Los Angeles Marine guilty of violating both section 8(a)(3) and section 8(a)(5). Quite unlike the Supreme Court, which a few years later expressed serious concern in the *First National Maintenance* decision for the economic problems of management, the Board seemed to go out of its way in *Los Angeles Marine* to reject such considerations, saying "the need to obtain economic relief from the terms of that [union] agreement...gives rise to the violation." The decision went on to hold that nothing could justify the action taken by Los Angeles Marine, which, the Board said, violated the provision in section 8(d) barring "midterm modification" of a union agreement. The argument (made also in *Milwaukee Spring I*) that the relocation did not "modify" the contract, but simply rendered it inoperative, was rejected, the Board holding that hiring new employees at a different location to do the same work at lower rates is as much a transgression of section 8(d) as it would be to lower the contract rates applicable to the employees at the old location, which section 8(d) clearly prohibits. To hold otherwise, the decision says, "would mean that employers would be permitted to achieve by indirection" what they may not "achieve by direct means under section 8(d)."[26]

The entire holding in *Los Angeles Marine* rested on the section 8(d) ruling, with the conduct of the company being described as an "unlawful effort to escape the economic impact of a binding agreement."[27] Thus the stage was set for *Milwaukee Spring.* The conflict between management's inherent right to run the business (except to the extent to which that right may be surrendered or abridged in the union contract) and the right of employees once they are covered by a union contract to continue to enjoy its benefits (or "fruits," as Mr. Lubbers will later describe them) is a classic one. Not surprisingly, it was resolved by the Carter Board in favor of workers' rights and against management rights in *Los Angeles Marine,* as it later was in *Milwaukee Spring I.* Neither decision is free of some degree of attenuation. In neither case did the Board make any effort to point to some actual term of the agreement which, in violation of section 8(d), was modified by the move and, of course, it could not have done so. There was none. What the Board did instead, in sweeping aside—if it was aware of them—the traditional understandings as to the nature and content of union agreements, was to *assume* that an ordinary union agreement confers on the employees in the bargaining unit defined in the agreement a *right* to perform the work upon which they are engaged. If such a right actually exists, it is unquestionably a job right of substantial consequence! The Board does not expound its right-to-the-work theory, but that is the clear import, we think, of its insistence that the employer cannot be permitted to "escape" his "obligations" under the union agreement.[28]

Provisions such as the Board assumed into the *Los Angeles Marine* agreement (sometimes called "work jurisdiction" or "work preservation" clauses) are by no means unheard of. Where they exist, however, they have been negotiated (i.e., traded for) and they are spelled out in detail in the union agreement. By treating the agreement in *Los Angeles Marine* as if it contained such a clause, the Board accomplished something else. In one expropriative stroke it gave to the union a veto power over one of the most basic of all managerial decisions: where shall the work be performed and by whom—a right traditionally deemed to be reserved to management *unless bargained away* (as it had not been in *Los Angeles Marine* and *Milwaukee Spring*) in union contract negotiations. The import of *Los Angeles Marine* (as more fully revealed by Mr. Lubbers in the quarterly report discussed below) is to require the employer to bargain back from the union, once it is in place, rights which have traditionally been regarded as vested in and remaining with management, as an incident of the ownership of the business, unless surrendered or abridged in the union negotiations.

The Board went further. Its treatment of the union agreement and the rights of the employees covered by it came very close to treating that agreement as though it were a common-law contract to employ. It is, of course, no such thing. An employment contract is an agreement of hire between an employer and an individual employee, pursuant to which the employer agrees to provide and the employee agrees to perform a specific job at an agreed wage for a specified time. The union agreement, on the other hand, is a *collective* agreement (the product of *collective* bargaining). It does not run between employer and employee, but between employer and union. It is not an undertaking *to employ* (and that status has never before been claimed for it[29]); it is simply an agreed-upon set of terms and conditions which will apply to members of the bargaining unit, *so long as there is a bargaining unit,* and only so long as there is work to be performed of the sort which the bargaining unit employees do. If it were otherwise—if the union agreement were, as the Board in *Los Angeles Marine* seemed to think, an undertaking to provide specific work to specific individuals for the life of the union agreement—an employer would never be able to lay off or terminate unneeded employees, something which is almost an everyday occurrence under nearly all union contracts.

The error into which the Carter Board fell in *Los Angeles Marine,* in treating the union agreement like an employment contract, is understandable given the philosophy of labor relations which informed that Board. To an agency concerned with employee rights—and, therefore, tending to take an overriding view of such rights—it might well seem unthinkable that employees who joined a union and who achieved through collective bargaining the benefits of a union wage scale should be deprived of such benefits—especially by the action of their employer, regardless of his economic motivations. But, understandable or not, the Board's view of what a union agreement is and what it does—in *Milwaukee Spring I,* as well as in *Los Angeles Marine*—is simply wrong, and, as we shall see, it was repudiated by the Reagan Board on traditional grounds.[30]

We mentioned that the Reagan Board repudiated *Los Angeles Marine,* as well as *Milwaukee Spring I.* It did so in the course of reconsidering the decision in *Milwaukee Spring I.* To understand why the Board took the unusual step of going back and specifically overruling a four-year-old case which was not before it, it is necessary to understand that *Los Angeles Marine* achieved landmark status by the way it was interpreted and exploited in *Milwaukee Spring I* and by General Counsel Lubbers before he left office. His treatment of the case in a quarterly report to the

Fanning Board, issued late in 1982, casts essential light on the state of the law with respect to job rights and management rights in work relocation cases as it confronted the Reagan Board when it commenced operation.

4. *The Lubbers Quarterly Report*

General Counsel Lubbers was well aware of the implications and uses of the doctrines promulgated in *Milwaukee Spring I* and *Los Angeles Marine*. Indeed, he no doubt helped to shape them by way of arguments and theories advanced by the Board's attorneys in the course of prosecuting unfair labor practice cases. Mr. Lubbers moved quickly after *Milwaukee Spring I* to flesh those ideas out by interpretation and, at the same time, to institutionalize them at the Board. The vehicle employed by the general counsel for that purpose was his quarterly report to the Board. The importance which Lubbers attached to the issue with which we are concerned is reflected in the fact that, late in 1982, he devoted one such report entirely to what he described as "cases dealing with relocation or subcontracting of unit work during the term of a contract with a union."[31] The "typical case" in this area of the law, Lubbers said, involved "an employer who, for economic reasons, sought modification of the labor cost provisions of the contract" and, if the union refused to consent, proceeded "to relocate or subcontract the unit work."[32]

We call attention at the outset to Lubbers's use of the term "unit work." As he (and others at the Board) used this term, and as unions have always used it, it is not simply descriptive—it is not just a way of identifying the work in question by associating it with a particular group of employees (the bargaining unit) who perform it. It is, rather, a statement that the work in question "belongs" to those employees, the members of the bargaining unit, and that they alone have the right to perform it. We have already indicated that we believe that this view of the ordinary union agreement (by "ordinary" we mean an agreement not containing language expressly conferring "work jurisdiction" on the union's members) is erroneous and at odds with most conventional thought concerning the union agreement and its legal effect. It is, nevertheless, important to stress the point, for such a view of the agreement reinforces the equally countertraditional and quite radical idea that, once a union is in place, the employer must bargain back from the union important aspects of his right to manage the business. That, of course, was the Lubbers thesis.

Mr. Lubbers's reference, in the quoted excerpt, to "labor cost provisions" is equally significant. In his view, there is something special about union labor costs. They are, as he sees it, inescapable once agreed to, unless the union consents to the escape. Such provisions, in the Lubbers view, follow the work and thus convert the union agreement into something like a contractual commitment to employ. We have already explained why we think this view of the union agreement is unsound,[33] yet it is just such a view that union agreements—and especially their labor costs—are somehow sacrosanct that pervaded the decisions in *Los Angeles Marine* and *Milwaukee Spring I*.

For that reason and by way, as we said earlier, of illuminating the thrust of the philosophy to which the Reagan Board will be addressing itself in this area of the law, we believe that the following brief statement of that philosophy, as expressed by Mr. Lubbers in the context of actual cases in which he elected to issue complaints, is highly instructive: "Just as the employer cannot [under section 8(d)] modify the contract, so too the employer cannot avoid the contract by the device of a mid-contract removal of the unit work to another location where the work will be performed at a cheaper labor cost."[34]

As we have already noted in our discussion of *Los Angeles Marine*, this interpretation of section 8(d) is simply wrong. It fails to distinguish between employer action taken in derogation of *actual terms* of a union contract (clearly not permitted under section 8(d) of the Act) and employer action taken pursuant to the inherent right of an owner to shut down or relocate at any time, provided that there are no explicit constraints upon that right embodied in the union agreement. He may have to bargain about it to impasse, but there is nothing in the ordinary union contract or in the Act itself which prevents his seeking to lower his labor costs by such action.

Not surprisingly, Mr. Lubbers was equally scornful of tradition when it came to management rights and the bargaining process:

> [A] clause *failing to prohibit* work transfer is not the same as a clause *affording an employer the right unilaterally to make* work transfers. As the Board has held, it is not incumbent on the union to obtain contract language supporting its statutory right; rather, *it is incumbent on the employer to obtain contract language* limiting or waiving that right. (Emphasis added.)[35]

It would be difficult to put more bluntly the radical and countertraditional idea that the employer has no inherent or residual rights and that, once a union is in place, he must bargain back from the union whatever rights he needs to continue the management of the business. This concept, it is true, did not originate with Mr. Lubbers, but it certainly flowered with him, although it died soon after (for the time being, at least) at the hands of the Reagan Board which proved both more knowledgeable about everyday labor-management affairs than Mr. Lubbers and more respectful of tradition.

One of the situations discussed by Mr. Lubbers in his quarterly report is of rather special interest, because it involves a move, to save on labor costs, *from one unionized facility to another.*[36] Thus it becomes clear that the Lubbers doctrine is not just one which protects unions, as such, against nonunion wage competition; it also protects one union against another when disparities in rate structures threaten one of the unions with deprivation of what Mr. Lubbers calls "the fruits of collective bargaining." This determination to protect unions, always and everywhere, against the normal economic consequences of their actions—including "too successful" bargaining—was a pervasive characteristic of what might be called the Lubbers era at the Board (1980-84), of which we now take our leave.

VII. The Board Changes—Again

1. *Introduction*

The stage is now set for the entry of a new Board majority and, consequently, a new interpretive philosophy with respect to many of the issues which we have been considering. It is not easy to date precisely the accession of a new Board or, at least, a new majority. The members' terms are staggered; they are for five years, one more year than a presidential term. They have to be approved by the Senate, and this frequently involves lengthy committee hearings which may or may not be followed by approval of the nominee. If a nominee is rejected, the process must begin again. This, in fact, happened in President Reagan's first term when the Senate Labor Committee refused to approve his nominee, John Van De Water, for chairman of the Board. Mr. Van De Water thereupon left the Board, on which he had been serving pending his confirmation. Ironically, this Reagan appointee had joined in the decision of *Milwaukee Spring I* which, as we shall see, was almost the first target of the Reagan Board majority once it got in place, which, by our reckoning, was by 1983.

Before turning to our analysis of the new Board's decisions, a few comments may not be inappropriate concerning these periodic realignments on the Board with the consequent tergiversations in decisional policies which result. Perhaps it is inevitable, with an administrative body whose members are appointed by the President in office at the time when the vacancy occurs, that they will reflect certain philosophical dispositions rather than others—rather, for example, than those of the appointing president's immediate predecessor (unless that was he). The NLRB historically has been a highly politicized agency, and perhaps that is unavoidable, given the subjects with which it deals. The members are charged (and they have been from the beginning) with conflicting ideologies and competing interests. Nevertheless, the periodic revisionist exercise is, in our judgment, no less regrettable for that.[1] Even if one approves of the "corrections" which, as we are about to see, the

Reagan Board applied in *Milwaukee Spring II,* the process is disturbing. Such periodic revisions and reversals of doctrine are purchased at a disturbing cost in the stability and predictability of the law—developments which cannot but disturb a lawyer who, even though his sympathies may be partisan, has a professional attachment to the rule of law.

2. Milwaukee Spring II[2]

The new Board majority quickly moved on the *Milwaukee Spring* case, which was still pending on appeal in the U.S. Court of Appeals for the Seventh Circuit. Not without some initial difficulty (for Mr. Lubbers was still in office), the Board managed to get the Court of Appeals to remand the case to it for additional consideration.[3]

With the case back before it, the Board quickly addressed itself to the holding which lay at the heart of *Milwaukee Spring I:* the company had unlawfully "modified" the union contract when, without the consent of the union, it relocated operations after bargaining over its proposed action had failed. This holding had embodied several corollary theories of law, not all of which were made explicit in *Milwaukee Spring I.* Their import and thrust, however, were perfectly clear to the Board which was reconsidering that decision. They were (1) that a union contract in and of itself constitutes a binding commitment by the employer, for the life of the contract, that the work performed by the employees covered by the contract belongs in some sense to them; (2) that such work may not, therefore, be assigned to other employees not members of that bargaining unit; and (3) that the pay rates under the union contract *attach* to such work so that, while the contract exists, that work may not be assigned elsewhere and performed at different rates by different employees.

As all labor relations professionals know, it is perfectly possible to negotiate and write into the union contract limitations of that sort on the employer and rights of that sort for the employees. The signal fact about *Milwaukee Spring I* was that this had not been done. Not only was there no such language in the union agreement but, in fact, as we have seen, there was language of a contrary tenor. It was contained in the contract's management clause. What the Board in *Milwaukee Spring I* had done was to disregard all this and to hold that (somehow) the union contract *in and of itself* stood as a bar to the assignment of the work elsewhere, and that the action to that end which the company had taken therefore constituted a "modification" of "terms and conditions" of the union contract in violation of section 8(d).

That entire rationale was firmly and explicitly rejected in *Milwaukee Spring II*. In the first place, said the Board: "[B]efore the Board may hold that Respondent violated Section 8(d), the Board first must identify a specific term 'contained in' the contract that the Company's decision to relocate modified."[4] And, in the absence of "terms" contained in the union agreement which abridge the employer's right to make the move which he seeks to make, then his obligation "remains the general one of bargaining in good faith to impasse over the subject before instituting the proposed change."[5]

The Board sweepingly rejected its predecessor's interpretation and application of section 8(d), including the idea that, upon the interposition of a union, the employer may no longer exercise the traditional rights of management unless he can bargain back from the union his right to act. This was a major reversal by the new Board, not just in decisional policy, but also in the philosophy espoused by its predecessor concerning workers' rights and management rights.

As we suggested in our earlier discussion, the traditional view has been that, even after employees have voted to be represented by a union, and even after the negotiation of a union contract, management retains all of its inherent rights and powers in respect of the running of the business, save to the extent that any such rights have been waived or limited in the union agreement. Decisions as to location of operations, methods and equipment to be employed, finance, marketing, and so forth, are thus the traditional prerogative of the owners and the managers of the enterprise, and they are not frequently abridged by the terms of a union contract.

The right to "direct the work force," to use the traditional phrase, is another such inherent and traditional right. It encompasses the right to determine the number and types of workers needed and to assign the work to them. These employment-related management rights are the ones which customarily are subject to *some* degree of abridgement by the union contract, e.g., by the application of seniority in such matters as layoffs, recalls, transfers, promotions, and vacations. To the extent not so abridged, however, these rights too have traditionally been deemed to remain with management.

It was no doubt this "inherent rights" principle that Justice Blackmun had in mind when he remarked, in *First National Maintenance,* upon FNM's "retained freedom to manage its affairs."[6] This is not to suggest that there is not a contrary view. Several decades ago, union proponents began to advance a theory of "inherent *union* rights." It argued that the moment employees select a union (even before any contract comes into being), management is barred from unilaterally acting upon wages, hours, or other terms or conditions of the now-unionized employees, and it can only regain the right to act by negotiating for it with the union (hence the phrase "bargain back," which we have used). Obviously, this theory conflicted in important respects with the theory of inherent management rights. More than that, in its more extreme form, it negated entirely the idea of *any* traditional or inherent reserved or retained rights of management. Indeed, so extreme was the form it took in *Milwaukee Spring I* and in the writings of Mr. Lubbers that it caused the Board in *Milwaukee Spring I* to ignore entirely some management rights language in *that* contract, which, at least arguably, permitted management to do what it did and was the result of precisely the kind of "bargaining back" which Mr. Lubbers appeared to demand.

In any case, it was these countertraditional theories that the Board in *Milwaukee Spring II* was now at pains to repudiate.

It will be recalled that there were two major thrusts in the rationale put forth in *Milwaukee Spring I*. They dealt, respectively, with the "right to do the work" and with "labor costs" under the union contract (i.e., the union rates). The Board in *Milwaukee Spring I* held that, in the absence of agreement by the union, the company was barred by section 8(d) of the Act (even after negotiating to impasse) from (a) moving the work to another location, and (b) having it performed there by other employees at lower rates. The Board in *Milwaukee Spring II* disagreed totally with that reasoning and that holding, saying:

> Respondent decided to transfer the assembly operations to a different plant where workers (who were not subject to the contract) would perform the work. In short, Respondent did not disturb the wages and benefits at its Milwaukee facility, and consequently did not violate Section 8(d) by modifying, without the Union's consent, the wage and benefits provisions contained in the contract.[7]

This, as we have indicated, accords with the traditional view of the union agreement. It is not an employment agreement, nor is it an absolute or unqualified ("all events") commitment to pay a wage. Rather, it is a contingent arrangement, the contingency being that the employer engages (or continues to engage) in operations at the location and with the workers covered by the agreement. We think (contrary, obviously, to Mr. Lubbers and his colleagues) that it is clear from the tone and language of the Act that it was intended that rights under the provisions of the Act (including the right to representation) could come into existence—and continue to exist—only so long as there was an employment in which the rights could apply.

Turning to the issue involving the relocation of the work, the Board in *Milwaukee Spring II* rejected the arguments (a) that the contract as a whole somehow implicitly gives members of the bargaining unit an indefeasible right to continue to perform the work (called "work jurisdiction" or "work preservation" when embodied in a union contract), and (b) that the contract's recognition clause had the effect of conferring such a right on the bargaining unit. As to the latter, the Board says it agrees with the courts in holding that there is "no basis for reading jurisdictional rights into standard clauses that merely recognized the contracts' coverage of specified employees."[8] More specifically, the Board went on, the recognition clause does not confer on the union or its members any right to keep the work which they have been performing in the original location. On this point, the Board says: "No doubt parties could draft such a clause; indeed, work-preservation clauses are commonplace. It is not for the Board, however, to create an implied work-preservation clause in every American labor agreement based on wage and benefits or recognition provisions, and we expressly decline to do so."[9]

The Board here does something more than merely to repudiate the Carter Board's erroneous interpretations of the *Milwaukee Spring* agreement as conferring a right to the work; it addresses itself to the broader concern that such an interpretation, if valid, would apply to all union agreements. It would have far-reaching impact on existing agreements, on the traditional assumptions and practices of management and union negotiators, and on the labor-management relationship as a whole. It is no doubt with this in mind that the Board elsewhere describes *Milwaukee Spring I* as a "radical departure."[10]

The Board then addresses the manner in which *Milwaukee Spring I* changed the rules, as they had earlier been understood to be, after the decision in *Ozark Trailers*.[11] Quoting from the decision in that case concerning the employer's freedom, after satisfying his bargaining duty, "to make and effectuate his decision," the Board notes that this "freedom" was nullified by its predecessor, first in *Los Angeles Marine* and then in *Milwaukee Spring I* (neither of which cases even mentioned *Ozark Trailers*). Indeed, says the Board, the decision in *Milwaukee Spring I* was a "substantial departure" from "NLRB textbook law" to the effect that "an employer need not obtain a union's consent on a matter not contained in the body of a collective bargaining agreement even though the subject is a mandatory subject of bargaining."[12] What the Board is

saying here accords with the traditional concept of management's reserved or retained rights discussed earlier: unless management has surrendered, or agreed to the abridgement of, one or more of its inherent
rights, then those rights are "retained" and may ordinarily be exercised
without the concurrence of the union. There may be, of course, an
obligation, as we have seen, to bargain over the *decision* to exercise the
right, but the bargaining need only proceed to impasse, and it need not
take place at all if the reservation of management rights is confirmed in
the contract's management clause.

The opinion in *Milwaukee Spring II* concludes with a section headed
"Realistic and Meaningful Collective Bargaining."[13] Under that
heading, the Board discusses the view which its predecessor had taken of
labor costs—as something special and as giving rise to a right in the
union under section 8(d) to block a relocation—and it finds such a view
counterproductive. If labor costs, when assigned as the reason for a
move, are to give rise to special restrictions on management, then
management would be likely to avoid assigning labor costs as the reason
for its move. Thus, possibly fruitful negotiations with the union would
never take place.

This seems a not unreasonable approach, as would be any other approach which favors candid discussion and productive negotiation as
against devious maneuvering and tests of power. As we see it, it can be
plausibly argued that labor costs under a union contract are, indeed,
"special," but only in this sense: if they are the *primary* reason for the
decision to relocate, then, under *First National Maintenance,* the decision is subject to mandatory bargaining as one of those which is directly
concerned with the employment relation. If they are not the reason for
the decision—if, for example, the motivating force is to seek some new
direction for the business or to redeploy capital—then the decision is not
subject to mandatory bargaining. Where the decision is partly based on
labor costs but primarily on purely business reasons, Justice Blackmun's
burden-benefits test comes into play.

The decision in *Milwaukee Spring II* was affirmed by the U.S. Court
of Appeals for the District of Columbia.[14] It would not serve any useful
purpose to attempt an analysis of the court's opinion. It is far from a
model of clarity and it betrays considerable (and, unfortunately, not uncommon) naivete concerning everyday labor-management affairs. What
is important from our standpoint is that the Court affirmed the holding
of the Board in *Milwaukee Spring II,* saying:

> Given that Milwaukee Spring acted without antiunion animus for
> purely economic reasons and fulfilled any statutory obligation to bar-

gain that it might have had, we hold that the Company did not violate Section 8(d) of the Act, either by offering to change its right to relocate for a midterm modification of the contract or by deciding to relocate when the Union rejected its modification proposals. The decision of the NLRB is *Affirmed.*[15]

We now turn to the next Board decision on plant closing which occurred. It was one in which the labor-costs factor was prominent.

3. *The* Otis Elevator *Case*[16]

This case has a curious procedural history—similar, in some ways, to *Milwaukee Spring.* A decision against the company was handed down by the Carter Board in March 1981.[17] It found Otis guilty of refusal to bargain over both the decision and the effects of a transfer of work from one plant to another and of refusing to provide information on the move to the union (the United Automobile Workers, the same union that was involved in *Milwaukee Spring*). Several months later, while the case was on appeal to the Court of Appeals for the D.C. Circuit, the Board asked the court to remand the case to it, so that it could reconsider its decision in the light of the intervening (June 1981) decision of the Supreme Court in the *First National Maintenance* case.

For reasons which are not clear (but which might have had something to do with the transition process at the Board), no decision was issued for two and one-half years. The transition accomplished, the Reagan Board, handed down its decision in *Otis* in April 1984, about two and one-half months after it had decided *Milwaukee Spring II.* Reversing the decision of its predecessor, the Board cleared the company of the charge of refusal to bargain over the decision and of the alleged refusal to supply information, but it remanded the case for further proceedings in connection with the alleged failure to engage in effects bargaining.

The case is of special interest, because the opinions (there were three in all, including a partial dissent) tell us a great deal about how the Reagan Board interprets *First National Maintenance* in respect of the duty to bargain over decisions and effects in plant relocation and other similar cases.

Otis Elevator Company had research and development operations located throughout the North American continent, including one at Mahwah, New Jersey, where employees were represented by the UAW, and another at Parsippany, New Jersey, where the employees were not represented by any union. Both locations did similar research and development work, but the larger one, Mahwah, was obsolescent and inadequate. For some time prior to 1975, Otis's share of the world market had been declining, and it was selling its products at less than cost merely to stay in the market. In addition, there was duplication of R & D work throughout its facilities.

In 1975, Otis was acquired by United Technologies of Hartford, Connecticut, whereupon a major review was made of Otis's technological status. The study showed, among other things, that Otis's technology was outdated. This was the reason for its noncompetitive position on world markets. In 1977, the conclusion was reached that the research and development operations at Mahwah and Parsippany should be shut down and the work consolidated at United Technologies' major R & D center at East Hartford, Connecticut. In connection with the move, construction on an Otis research center, to cost approximately three million dollars, was begun at East Hartford and was scheduled for completion in 1979.

The Board's decision does not disclose what contacts (if any) there were between Otis and the union at Mahwah at the time when the decision was finally made and its implementation begun. In any case, the union charged that Otis failed to bargain over its decision and over the effects of its decision on the employees (both those who were transferred to East Hartford and those who remained at Mahwah) and that Otis refused to make available to the union the study which dictated the relocation action.

Although on the facts (including the absence of any charge of anti-union animus) the case seems clear-cut, the Carter Board had decided against Otis, holding that there was a mandatory duty to bargain over the decision and its effects. The Reagan Board disagreed. Because of the importance of *Otis* to our assessment of where the law currently stands, as well as where it is likely to go, we examine this decision, particularly the Board members' discussions of the applicable law, in some detail.

The Board opened its opinion—even before it stated the facts of the case—with these comments concerning the applicable law:

> Respondent was free to decide to discontinue its research and development activities in Mahwah, New Jersey, and to consolidate them with its operations in East Hartford, Connecticut, unrestrained by Section 8(a)(5) and 8(d) of the Act. Acknowledging that this decision touched on a matter of central concern to the union and to the employees it represented, we nevertheless find under the guidance of *First National Maintenance* that the decision turned not upon labor costs, but instead turned upon a change in the nature and direction of a significant facet of its business. Thus, it constituted a managerial decision of the sort

which is at the core of entrepreneurial control outside the limited scope of Section 8(d).[18]

We conclude that the Respondent's decision to discontinue its research and development functions at Mahwah, New Jersey, and to transfer those functions to its facility in East Hartford, Connecticut, was not subject to mandatory bargaining.[19]

Before explaining why, the Board quotes the "balancing test" from *First National Maintenance:*

> Management must be free from the constraints of the bargaining process to the extent essential for the running of a profitable business. …In view of an employer's need for unencumbered decisionmaking, bargaining over management decisions that have a substantial impact on the continued availability of employment should be required only if the benefit, for labor management relations and the collective-bargaining process, outweighs the burden placed on the conduct of the business.[20]

The Board then states that the management decision in this case was aimed at improving the business and did not turn on labor costs.[21] Therefore, says the Board:

> Despite the evident effect on employees the critical factor to a determination whether the decision is subject to mandatory bargaining is the essence of the decision itself, i.e., whether it turns upon a change in the nature or direction of the business, or turns upon labor costs—*not* its effect on employees nor a union's ability to offer alternatives. The decision at issue here clearly turned upon a fundamental change in the nature and direction of the business, and thus was not amenable to bargaining.[22]

It is interesting to note that the Board does not say simply that the decision was not "subject to" bargaining; it says that it is not "amenable" to bargaining, thus putting a slightly different spin on that term than we have seen heretofore. Amenability is now to be measured by the *nature of the decision,* not (as Mr. Lubbers would have had it) by whether it would be *possible* to bargain about it.

The Board devotes an entire section of its opinion to a discussion of section 8(d), remarking that, prior to *First National Maintenance,* the Board had applied its mandatory bargaining requirement to plant closure and other managerial decisions which affected the *direction of the business,* as well as the employees. The Board says bluntly: "The Court's opinion rejected that approach." And then it goes on to say: "The Court's view that predictability in this area is necessary for both labor and management leads us to elaborate on our present view of Section 8(d) as it impacts upon management decisions, other than partial closings, to change the nature of the enterprise."[23]

In the exposition which then follows, the Board turns first to the much-discussed footnote 22 in *First National Maintenance* in which the Supreme Court had said that it "intimate[d] no view concerning [the application of mandatory decision bargaining to] relocations, sales, other kinds of subcontracting, automation, etc." The Board says that in those matters it will, like the Court in *First National Maintenance,* turn to Justice Stewart. It quotes his language (379 U.S. at 223) to the effect that management decisions may "imperil job security, or indeed terminate employment entirely" (citing investment in labor-saving machinery or the liquidation of a business as circumstances which might have such an effect) and adds his oft-quoted statement that "[n]othing the Court holds today should be understood as imposing a duty to bargain collectively regarding such managerial decisions, which lie at the core of entrepreneurial control."

The Board continues its quotation of Justice Stewart to the effect that management decisions "concerning the commitment of investment capital and the basic scope of the enterprise are not in themselves primarily about conditions of employment," and, being decisions "which are fundamental to the basic direction of the corporate enterprise or which impinge only indirectly upon employment security, [they] should be excluded from" the purview of section 8(d). The Board adds: "Thus, for the reasons the Court gave in *First National Maintenance* (inter alia, management's need for predictability, flexibility, speed, secrecy, and to operate profitably), we hold that excluded from Section 8(d) of the Act are decisions which affect the *scope, direction or nature of the business.*"[24] In a footnote, the Board adds:

> Such decisions include, inter alia, decisions to sell a business or a part thereof, to dispose of its assets, to restructure or to consolidate operations, to subcontract, to invest in labor-saving machinery, to change the methods of finance or of sales, advertising, product design, and all other decisions akin to the foregoing.[25]

Thus the Board uses the guidance provided by *First National Maintenance* to answer the questions which the Court itself had left open in footnote 22. As we indicated in our discussion of that case, this seemed to be what the Court had in mind, although Mr. Lubbers and the Carter Board were not disposed to see it that way.

Even subcontracting decisions, the Board says (noting the "almost reflexive" response of past Boards in ordering mandatory decision bargaining in such cases), must be subjected to the test of whether they are primarily about labor costs (and, therefore, directly concern the employment relationship) or are based on some business reason.[26]

Obviously, it is this Board's intention to free genuine *business* decision making from (in the language of *First National Maintenance*) the "constraints of the bargaining process." The freedom is not to be total, however. Although decisions based on labor costs under a union agreement are as much "business decisions" as any others, the Board intends to treat "labor costs" differently—but not so drastically differently as its predecessor did. Accordingly, while the Board will hold (as demonstrated in the foregoing excerpts) that decisions concerning the scope, direction, or nature of the business are to be excluded from the bargaining requirements of section 8(d), this will not be the case in respect of decisions which "turn upon" a need to reduce labor costs. Those decisions, the Board says (again in harmony with *First National Maintenance,* as we read it), are within the mandatory bargaining requirements of section 8(d). As the Board says: "Included within Section 8(d), however, in accordance with the teachings of *Fibreboard,* are all decisions which turn upon a reduction of labor costs. This is true whether the decision may be characterized as subcontracting, reorganizing, consolidation or relocation."[27] The Board here makes an interesting remark by way of illustrating the foregoing. Even if there had not been a stipulation in *Milwaukee Spring* to the effect that the decision there was a mandatory subject of bargaining, the Board says nevertheless "we would have so held."[28]

The Board then returns to *First National Maintenance* and the remark of the Court that if a failing business is deciding to close and labor costs are an important factor, then management will have "an incentive to confer voluntarily," but this does not necessarily put the *decision* within section 8(d). Instead, if labor costs are a factor in the total situation of a faltering business, that element of the problem can be adequately dealt with, as the Court suggested in *First National Maintenance,* in the course of effects bargaining. The Board adds, "We discern no substantial reason why this analysis is not equally applicable to other decisions which turn upon a significant change in the nature or direction of a business."[29]

What the Board is saying here provides, we think, a clue to how it will handle future cases in which there is an overriding *business* purpose for the decision, and yet the impact of the decision on employment, although secondary, is such that the union has a legitimate and, in the words of Justice Blackmun, a "central and pressing concern" over the jobs involved. The Board *might* impose decision bargaining if the burden-benefits test comes out that way, but, as we have already observed, that result is not too likely when the *business* thrust of the decision is primary and strong. In such a case, however, the interest of the union and its members could be handled in the course of the effects bargaining which the Board can require pursuant to section 8(d) as interpreted in *First National Maintenance.* Whether it *will,* in every such case, require such bargaining is not clear, as will appear from the remainder of our discussion of the case, but, as that discussion also discloses, the odds seem to favor it.

The principal opinion in *Otis Elevator* concludes at this point. The Board's disposition of the case, as we noted at the outset, was that the charges based on refusal to bargain over the decision, and on the refusal to supply information in connection therewith, should be dismissed. As to the remaining charge that Otis committed a refusal to bargain over the *effects* of the consolidation on the employees transferred from Mahwah, as well as on those who remained, the Board remanded this aspect of the case for further proceedings before the administrative law judge, who had decided it in the first instance, with directions to consider the question remanded "in light of our decision today."[30]

Only two members of the Board—Chairman Donald Dotson and Member Robert Hunter (no longer on the Board)—signed the opinion which we have been discussing. Member Don Zimmerman (whose term expired several months later) concurred in part and dissented in part, and Member Dennis filed a lengthy concurring opinion. Both separate opinions—and particularly that of Member Dennis—are of assistance to us in trying to assess and predict the new directions in which the law on plant closures and relocations is moving. Moreover, since the vote of Member Dennis was necessary to make the majority in *Otis Elevator,* her opinion needs to be read with the principal opinion, if we are to comprehend the full holding of the case.

Member Dennis states at the outset of her opinion that, although she agrees with the result reached by Chairman Dotson and Member Hunter, "I do not rely on their rationale." She prefers, she says, to rely on her own analysis of the *First National Maintenance* case, and she thereupon sets forth that analysis in detail. It is a thorough and painstaking job. Since it parallels, to a substantial degree, our own analysis of that case, we find ourselves largely in agreement with it. For that reason we shall not repeat here in detail Member Dennis's analysis of *FNM*.[31] Instead, we proceed to what seems to us a more useful exercise: an examination of the criteria for decision which Member Dennis draws from her study of *FNM*. These are stated in her concurring opinion under the heading "A Framework for Analyzing Category III Decisions," which begins as follows:

> Based on the foregoing examination of the *First National Maintenance* opinion, I shall apply the following analysis in cases raising the issue of whether bargaining should be required over Category III management decisions (i.e., decisions that have a direct impact on employment, but have as their focus only the economic profitability of the employer's operation). These decisions include, without limitation, the following: Plant relocations, consolidations, automation, and subcontracting.[32]

Member Dennis appends to the foregoing a footnote which states:

> Of course, if the matter presented is an economically motivated partial closing or a sale, no decision bargaining is required. *First National Maintenance* and prior Board precedent strike the balance in favor of no duty to bargain about such decisions. *U.S. Contractors,* 257 NLRB 1180 (1981), petition for review denied 697 F. 2d 692 (5th Cir. 1983) (partial closing); *General Motors Corp.,* 191 NLRB 951 (1971), petition for review denied sub nom. *Auto Workers Local 864 v. NLRB,* 470 F. 2nd 422 (D.C. Cir. 1972) (sale). Partial closing and sale decisions necessarily involve management's "retained freedom to manage its affairs unrelated to employment." *First National Maintenance,* 452 U.S. at 677.[33]

Member Dennis then turns to the application of her analysis to the *Otis* situation. Clearly, she says, it is a "Category III" case and hence "the first step is to examine the factors underlying the Respondent's decision and determine whether any factor within the union's control was a significant consideration in the Respondent's decision."[34] She concludes that none was. As she puts it, "There was nothing that the Union could have offered that reasonably could have affected management's decision."[35] After highlighting the facts supporting the foregoing statement (including the facts that the company's problems were problems of technology, facilities, and geography), she says:

> I therefore find that the Respondent's decision to consolidate its research and development functions in East Hartford was not amenable to resolution through collective bargaining, and on that basis join my

colleagues in dismissing the complaint allegation that the Respondent unlawfully refused to bargain with the union over the decision.

And then she adds, sharply departing from the Carter Board-Lubbers philosophy (and from dissenting Member Zimmerman, as we shall see):

> I hasten to point out, however, that in the context of my analytical framework a finding that a decision *is* amenable to resolution through collective bargaining will not automatically result in a determination that bargaining over the decision is mandatory. For, in that situation, bargaining will be required "*only if* the benefit, for labor-management relations and the collective-bargaining process, outweighs the burden placed on the conduct of the business." (Emphasis is Member Dennis's.)[36]

In other words, the mere fact that a decision *can* be bargained about does not mean that it *must* be bargained about, and this does seem to be what Justice Blackmun had in mind when he made his balancing test applicable even to those "decisions that have a substantial impact on the continued availability of employment." Addressing herself specifically to the labor costs issue, Member Dennis adds:

> Even when labor costs are a significant consideration the analytical framework mandates balancing the "benefit" against the "burden," obligating the General Counsel to prove that the amenability of the decision to resolution through the bargaining process outweighs the constraints bargaining places on management. Such a showing would be difficult here because the burden elements are substantial.[37]

Member Dennis shows special sensitivity to the "burden" aspect. Earlier in her lengthy opinion, she reviewed a number of federal courts of appeal decisions in which the Board's decision-bargaining rulings were rejected, and she relates them to the burden-benefits test, finding in each that the court refused to enforce a mandatory decision-bargaining order on the (at least implicit) ground that such bargaining would be a burden because of the overriding economic necessities of the business situation.[38] Member Dennis concluded her survey of the cases by saying: "I stress that these burden elements cut across all sorts of Category III decisions. Where the burden elements in a particular case are weighty, as illustrated above, it is likely that the decision at issue will not be a mandatory subject of bargaining."[39] As already noted, Member Dennis concurred fully in the disposition of the *Otis* case as set forth in what she calls "the plurality opinion."

Member Zimmerman (a holdover from the "old" Board) predictably dissented, but only in part. He concurred in the majority ruling that the employer had no duty to bargain in respect of the transfer from Mahwah to East Hartford, but he did so on the ground that there was no way in which the union could have helped the situation, and, therefore, the issue was not "amenable to resolution through collective bargaining."[40] Member Zimmerman, however, differs from the other members of the Board, including Member Dennis. If the decision *had been* amenable to collective bargaining, he would order it, whereas she would not—not until the situation had also been subjected to the burden-benefits test.

Member Zimmerman further stated that he would have adhered to the earlier Board decision in *Otis* (which had ordered effects bargaining), rather than remanding the case for a hearing on that issue, as the majority here does. Member Zimmerman makes it clear, in fact, that he would order effects bargaining in all cases, and the Board majority in *Otis* was just as clearly willing to order effects bargaining in that case, as its remand of the case for a resolution of that issue demonstrated, even though it had held that decision bargaining was not required.[41]

This gives rise to some interesting questions concerning effects bargaining, and we might as well digress at this point to raise them and deal with them. Is effects bargaining only *derivative* from an obligation (or a possible obligation) to bargain over the decision, or does it stand independently? To put it another way: Is effects bargaining only ancillary to decision bargaining and, therefore, applicable only in those cases in which decision bargaining is imposed (either outright or following the balancing test) or does it apply to all cases, even those in which decision bargaining cannot conceivably be ordered, such as Member Dennis's "Category I" cases, where the impact on employment is so "indirect and attenuated" (in Justice Blackmun's phrase) that mandatory bargaining over such a decision would be wholly inappropriate and is not required by the Act? Can there, nevertheless, be an effects-bargaining obligation in such situations?

These are no idle philosophical questions, for, as Justice Blackmun observed, a great deal of what unions would seek to achieve in decision bargaining can also be achieved in effects bargaining. The contribution of the concept, therefore, to workers' rights in closing situations would be far from inconsequential. There are strong (although not necessarily legalistic) arguments to be made for requiring effects bargaining in all or almost all cases. It provides, among other things, an amelioration of the impact of even a purely business-motivated shutdown on the employees involved. It eliminates the "runaway" flavor in such situations and replaces it with a demonstration that the employer means to deal fairly with the legal representative of his employees.

At the same time, however, it must be acknowledged that many of the factors which argue against the imposition of a decision-bargaining requirement (the need for speed and secrecy, for example) would argue as well against effects bargaining in many situations. This is particularly true in light of the fact that effects bargaining (like decision bargaining) is supposed to take place before the decision has been implemented.

On the other hand, Justice Blackmun was quite explicit that only "the decision itself" was outside the statutory ambit of mandatory bargaining in the *First National Maintenance* case. He made it equally clear that the effects-bargaining obligation remained, i.e., that "effects" were "terms and conditions" under section 8(d). Indeed, effects bargaining had been engaged in by First National Maintenance and the union while the case was making its way to the Supreme Court.[42] Had it not been, the Court would surely have ordered it. And it very likely would do so in other balancing test cases in which decision bargaining was held not to be required.

Does this mean that effects bargaining can also be required in "Category I" cases—those in which, by definition, decision bargaining is ruled out *ab initio?* We think the answer is that it can be and, in many cases, it probably will be. There seems to be no difference in principle between the case in which decision bargaining is ruled out after the balancing test and one in which it is ruled out without any test. If the effects-bargaining obligation survives in the former case, there is no reason, we think, why it should not persist in the latter. And, if we are right, the workers' right conferred by section 8(a)(5) extends to more situations than might have been thought. Certainly, it is a remedy which unions can seek, and which management can reject only at some risk.

Now it is true that effects bargaining does not afford unions the bargaining leverage they have in decision bargaining, where management is precluded from proceeding until the duty to bargain has, one way or another, been discharged. At the same time, the employer may not put it off indefinitely or convert it into an empty exercise, for Justice Blackmun warned that effects bargaining must be conducted "in a meaningful manner and at a meaningful time." The results for the employees (at least in some cases) will not be substantially different from what would have been achieved had decision and effects bargaining both been pursued.[43] Indeed, an argument could be made for requiring effects bargaining even in a total shutdown (going-out-of-business) case, but for the fact that the Court in *Darlington* foreclosed that by holding such situations to be completely beyond the reach of the Act. It is, perhaps, superfluous (but it will serve to bring this digression on effects bargaining to a close) to add that no effects bargaining—indeed, no bargaining of any kind—can be required if the *union agreement,* in one way or another, handles the issue of bargaining in a plant-closing or plant-relocation situation.

4. *The* Gar Wood-Detroit *Case*

First National Maintenance changed the emphasis in decision-bargaining cases by insisting on the importance of the *nature* of the decision in determining whether or not it should be subjected to mandatory decision bargaining. If the focus of the decision was the *business,* then, even though it might have significant impact on employees and their jobs, the duty to bargain over the decision did not apply. *Otis Elevator* emphasized this new approach by remarking that this "essence of the decision" test would apply even in contracting-out cases. *Fibreboard,* in other words (as Justice Stewart had pointed out), did not indiscriminately make *all* contracting-out decisions the subject of mandatory bargaining. Only those in which, like that case, the management decision "turns on" labor costs or other matters integral to the employment relationship are to be subjected to mandatory bargaining.

Within a year, the Board got an opportunity to apply that reasoning in *Gar Wood-Detroit Truck Equipment, Inc.,* which the Board decided on February 19, 1985.[44] The company was a small one and its business consisted of installing pieces of specialized equipment (e.g., snowplows, scrapers, lights, and horns) on trucks owned by its customers, using its own cranes, compressors, and the like. The relationship between the company and the union was a long-standing one and there was no question of any antiunion animus. There was also no question that the company was in serious financial straits by 1981. At that time, in the course of contract renewal negotiations, the company sought relief, but the union (again the Auto Workers) refused, even though union employment at the company had dropped precipitately over a three-year period so that by 1981 most of the former eight-man work force was on layoff.

Gar Wood decided to get out of the installation and service business. Two men, Essig and Childress, who had previously performed work for the company on a subcontract basis offered to take over the installation and service work and to continue to perform it on the company's premises as independent contractors, using Gar Wood's equipment. An agreement was worked out pursuant to which the company leased its facilities and equipment to Essig and Childress, who also agreed to pay part of the company's rent and utility costs. Under the agreement, Gar Wood had no right to exercise any control over the employees of Essig and Childress.[45]

The company had not informed the union of its new arrangement, and it did not bargain over or otherwise discuss its decision with the union. After the agreement was reached, the company duly notified the union of the agreement and the consequent elimination of the service and mounting departments and the termination of the employees (all but one were by then on layoff-status) who had formerly worked in those operations. At that point, the union filed a grievance, but it also now offered, for the first time, to make concessions. The company found the union's offer inadequate, although it had several meetings with the union concerning possible expedients for getting the union's laid off members back to work. The talks were fruitless, and a few months later, in April 1982, the union filed charges that the company's failure to bargain over the contracting-out decision violated section 8(a)(5) of the Act. In the subsequent proceeding, the Board argued that the case was governed by *Fibreboard,* while the company argued that it was a "partial closing" and that *First National Maintenance* applied.

The case came before an administrative law judge early in 1983.[46] He found the situation to be governed by *Fibreboard,* because it involved simply the replacement of employees with those of an independent contractor to do the same work. He also found the subject matter amenable to collective bargaining, and he recommended a *Fibreboard*-type order: The company must reinstitute the discontinued operations and reinstate the terminated employees with back pay, while proceeding to carry out its bargaining obligations concerning the decision and its effects.

The Board's decision was handed down early in 1985, by which time the Reagan Board was firmly in the saddle. On the *Fibreboard* point, the Board rejected the reasoning of the administrative law judge and held that the contracting out "turned not on labor costs but on a significant change in the nature and direction of the company's business" and that there was, therefore, no duty to bargain about the decision. This, of course, threw out the ALJ's recommended order that the operations be reinstituted.

The Board agreed with the ALJ, however, that the company had a duty to bargain over the *effects* of its decision, which it had failed to fulfill.[47]

Member Dennis concurred in part and dissented in part. She disagreed with the majority over the decision-bargaining obligation, and since she is an important component of the "new majority," we need to examine her reasoning[48] if we are to be able to predict with any certainty where the Board is likely to come out in future cases involving decision bargaining in plant closures and similar situations.

Member Dennis agreed with the majority that the company was obligated to engage in effects bargaining, but she also felt that the employer could have and should have bargained over the decision. Her reasoning follows what she calls the two-step test that she applied in the *Otis Elevator* case. The first step in that test is to determine whether the management decision was amenable to collective bargaining (i.e., whether any of the significant factors in the decision was something that the union could do something about). Member Dennis felt that the union in *Gar Wood* "could have made offers that reasonably could have affected management's decision" (ignoring the fact that the union in the *Gar Wood* case had passed up several opportunities to do just that). But thus deciding in favor of amenability (which would have been enough in the days of the Carter Board and Mr. Lubbers) is not enough now. The second step for Member Dennis is to apply the *FNM* burden-benefits test. Member Dennis goes about this in a curious way. She decides (unlike the Board majority) that the action of Gar Wood did not constitute a significant change in the direction of the business. Rather (like the ALJ) she sees it as essentially a substitution situation, like *Fibreboard*. From this she argues that "the benefit achieved by subjecting the [company's] decision to the bargaining process outweighs any burdens placed on management." This seems somewhat of a *non sequitur,* and the confusion is not allayed by her use of the word "benefit" in a sort of free-floating manner, not modified by Justice Blackmun's qualifications (benefit for "labor-management relations and the collective bargaining process"). Member Dennis may feel that *any* engagement in collective bargaining is a benefit to labor-management relations, but this is a proposition which would not command universal assent. She also seems to feel that it can be taken for granted that it is not an undue burden on a business to have to bargain over decisions which (as in *Fibreboard*) are not of a sort which affect the "nature and direction" of the business. Again, the proposition seems at least debatable.

On the other hand, Member Dennis's conclusion—that the case is sufficiently analogous to *Fibreboard* to demand the same remedy—has a good deal to commend it. She seems to come to a sound conclusion, notwithstanding a certain lack of clarity in her expression of her reasoning. Where does this leave us?

Decision-bargaining orders will continue to be far fewer than before, but contracting-out situations will still, on account of *Fibreboard,* present a strong case for requiring decision bargaining, with this possible exception: if the contracting out is not a simple substitution of employees and if the work is thereafter to be performed *off the premises,* a decision-bargaining order might not be forthcoming, since the arrangement will tend to seem more like a change in the nature or direction of the business.

That concludes our discussion of the cases. It is time now to take stock.

5. *Workers' Rights Under the National Labor Relations Act— A Summary*

We began our examination of the National Labor Relations Act as a source of workers' rights in plant-closing situations by remarking that in the current debate over that issue the Act appears to have been slighted.[49] Yet, as we have been seeing, the Act has been interpreted to give rise to rights considerably more substantive in character than anything envisioned by, for example, the so-called plant-closing laws. This has been accomplished primarily through the sections defining the employer unfair labor practices of (a) discouraging membership in unions, and (b) refusing to bargain collectively and in good faith. With respect to the latter, section 9(a) of the Act provides that ''[r]epresentatives designated or selected for the purposes of collective bargaining by the majority of the employees in a unit appropriate for such purposes shall be the exclusive representative of all the employees in such unit for the purposes of collective bargaining.''

Section 8(d) defines the duty to bargain collectively as ''the performance of the mutual obligation of the employer and the representative of the employees to meet at reasonable times and confer in good faith with respect to wages, hours, and other terms and conditions of employment.'' Section 8(a)(5) makes it an unfair labor practice for an employer ''to refuse to bargain collectively with the representatives of his employees.''

Several interpretations of these provisions are relevant:

(1) To ''refuse'' to bargain includes *failing* to bargain (or failing to afford a union an opportunity to bargain) in circumstances in which the Board deems that a duty to bargain exists. Failure to bargain also includes a failure to bargain in ''good faith,'' as the Board adjudges it.

(2) The duty to bargain includes a duty on the part of the employer, once a union representative has been ''designated or selected,'' to

refrain from acting unilaterally (i.e., without bargaining or offering to bargain) in respect of wages, hours, or other terms and conditions of the employment of any represented employee.

(3) The duty to bargain is not confined to "wages, hours, and other terms and conditions of employment" as such. It extends to *any managerial action* which *affects* any of those things. This includes action which, by closing or moving the plant where the jobs existed, eliminates the jobs and the wages and other conditions attached to them.

(4) From the foregoing, it follows that the management *decisions* which lead to job elimination become subjects of bargaining.

Thus we see that under the rubric of collective bargaining—particularly the right to bargain over terms and conditions of employment—the Act confers on employees a right to intervene and, to a considerable degree, to participate in the managerial decision-making process. Acting through their unions and the collective bargaining process (and provided with leverage by way of the right to strike), employees can discuss and delay decisions which would eliminate their jobs. They can put a price (in terms of severance arrangements) on the implementation of such decisions. They may even persuade the employer to reconsider and reverse his proposed course of action. True, this right falls short (owing to the nature of collective bargaining under our law) of full participation in the sense of being able to block or veto the decision. The union's assent is not an indispensable condition to the implementation of the management decision. Bargaining in good faith to impasse is all that the Act requires of the employer. Nevertheless, the workers' right is substantial and meaningful, because it carries with it the ability to impose some (perhaps considerable) costs on decisions to eliminate jobs, and, consequently, it carries with it the potential ability to cause the modification or revocation of such decisions.

Nor is bargaining over managerial decisions the only source from which workers' rights may be derived under the Act. Union contract negotiations offer a wide range of possibilities for the creation of employee rights in the job. The possible issue of contracting out work, for example, can be (indeed, in the automobile industry these days it quite regularly is) handled in contract negotiations. Contracting out can be prohibited for the duration of the agreement (i.e., the employer can surrender his right to take that course) or its use by the employer can be conditioned in various ways which diminish its impact on his employees.

Similarly, the possibility of plant relocation can be handled by contract clauses which either prohibit or restrict removal of the operation for the life of the contract or which permit the employees (and their union wage rates) to "follow the work."

In addition, union contracts can provide for reopening during their term, in order to permit negotiation to deal, *ad hoc,* with closing or removal situations which could not have been anticipated when the contract was negotiated. The possibilities of dealing with change, anticipated or unanticipated, in short, are many and varied because of the flexibilities of collective bargaining and the bargaining process. These, however, are *voluntary* aspects of collective bargaining. The principal focus of our treatment of the law here has been on its *compulsory* aspects —the way in which employers are *required* by the Act to bargain over their decisions and over the impact of those decisions on employees and jobs and how that converts to "workers' rights" in respect of the job.

We noted at the outset of this study the tensions between workers' rights and management rights. To some extent, the one can only expand or be fostered or protected at the expense of the other. The implications of this were lost for a long time on the Board or, at any rate, were of no concern to it. We have traced the Board's decisional history from an era when its total preoccupation was with the rights of employees under the Act to an era in which, guided by the Supreme Court, it acknowledges a duty to consider management rights as well and to interpret and apply the Act in a manner designed to accommodate the two. As we have just suggested, the latter-day emphasis on management rights (and management's problems in running the business) is necessarily purchased at some cost to workers' rights as the Board earlier expounded them. A summary of where the law now stands, therefore, is best framed in terms of what the law does and does not require of employers, for it is out of those requirements—out of the elements of the employer's duty to bargain over his plant-closing decision—that the workers' right in a plant-closing situation arises.

As we see it, the following propositions emerge from the decisions of the United States Supreme Court and the decisions of the Board, including those of the Reagan Board, concerning a management decision to shut down or relocate a plant:

A. The decision *must* be bargained about if the reason for the decision is the cost of operating under a union contract (e.g., wages, restrictive work rules, etc.).

B. The decision *need not* be bargained about if the reason is a business one (e.g., obsolete plant, loss of market, financial losses, etc.).

C. If the decision is partly due to business conditions and partly due to labor costs, it will not have to be bargained about if the business reason is dominant, but it will have to be bargained about if the labor cost factor predominates.

Paragraph C represents our attempt to assess how the balancing test will work out in practice. Obviously, the concept of "amenability" (defined both as the susceptibility of an issue to being bargained about and the ability and willingness of the union and its members to do something about it) plays a role in both C and A above.

In all three of the categories listed above, there is an effects-bargaining obligation—actual in the cases of A and C, potential (but probable) in the case of B. But whether the bargaining is over effects or over the decision itself, it need not be carried on beyond the point of impasse.

Finally, we remind the reader of the *Darlington* principle: there need be no bargaining of any sort over a shutdown which is a total going out of business for the enterprise.

As shown by the foregoing summary, the concept of workers' rights under the Act is not what it was seen to be in the days of *Ozark Trailers* and *Los Angeles Marine* and Mr. Lubbers. It has been diminished by the Supreme Court's insistence on the accommodation of management rights, but it remains significant. For example, a union's right to be bargained with in plant-closing situations can be converted into substantial rights for its members by way of severance pay provisions, transfer rights to another operation of the same employer, or even a modification or revocation of the shutdown decision. In addition, the statutory right to bargain in regular contract negotiations, for terms and conditions that afford protection or indemnity in the event of a plant-closing decision, can also yield significant rights-in-the-job. True, none of these actually amounts to a genuine *property right* in the job, but, as we are about to see, that notion is pretty much a chimera in any case.

VIII. Job Rights and The Common Law

1. *Introduction: Some Definitions and Principles*

We conclude this study by inquiring whether, plant-closing laws and the National Labor Relations Act aside, there are job rights[1] to be found elsewhere in the law. Before doing so, we shall dispose quickly and finally of the idea (to which we have had occasion to allude in several earlier contexts) that workers have, or acquire over time, a property right in a job simply by holding that job. This terminology, fairly widely used, has done much to muddy the job rights debate. A genuine, substantive property (i.e., ownership) right, in the sense that the possessor of it cannot be displaced from his job without his assent (and that is what a "property right" literally would mean), is so rare as to be, for all practical purposes, nonexistent.

In lieu of a dissertation on why this is so and on how property rights are acquired and transferred in a contractarian, property-based system like ours, we offer a few brief illustrations: (1) When I hire a chauffeur to drive my automobile, he does not thereby acquire a property right in my car or in its steering wheel, no matter how long and how devotedly he does the job. (2) A young man employed as an associate lawyer by a law firm gains an ownership status only when he becomes a partner. But, by definition, he is at that point no longer an employee. Indeed, about the only *employee* situation in which it might be said that there is something like a property right in the job is the case of an actor or actress with a run-of-the-play contract. Even in that case, however, if the producer is willing to pay damages for breach of contract, he probably can replace the star. Moreover—and very much to the point—the producer can decide to close the play, and there is nothing the star can do about it. The star has no such right to perform the role (right-in-the-job) as will permit him or her to compel the producer to keep the play running. Yet it is something very like such a right that pure "property rights" advocates argue for—vainly, in our judgment. Even an employee who acquires an ownership right in the enterprise through a stock ownership plan or an employee buy-out can be laid off, if the business demands it. Indeed, the property right-in-the-job theory is so utterly without a rational basis that, as we have gone along, we have come to believe that the property rights terminology probably has been adopted by job rights advocates more for polemical purposes than for the purpose of signifying anything like a true ownership right in the job.[2] Whatever its value to job rights advocates, we urge that the "property rights" terminology be abandoned. It is, as we have seen, misleading. It generates undue opposition. And it does nothing to further the debate in any productive direction.

But the fact that job rights do not involve true property rights does not dispose of the issue. There are a variety of rights—some the product of common law, others the product of the employment arrangement or the union contract—which can be described, entirely legitimately, as "job rights." Some are substantive, some are procedural. On the substantive side, there are, for example, union contract clauses that, when successfully negotiated by a union, accord to its members so-called job jurisdiction (i.e., the right of a particular classification of employees to perform a particular type of work if and when that work is required) or clauses which provide that the union contract will cover the employer's work wherever it may be performed. Such provisions are in addition to such somewhat more frequent job rights provisions as seniority in the event of layoffs, which guarantees some employees the right to remain at work longer than others. These are not all the "terms and conditions" which might be considered to be "job rights," but they are the most relevant and illustrative for our purpose.

A further source of job rights can be found in the decisions of labor arbitrators. Construing union contracts in the course of deciding grievance arbitration issues, labor arbitrators have often found in the union contract restrictions on, for example, the right of management to eliminate or combine jobs or to transfer work—restrictions which are not spelled out in the contract, but which the arbitrator "implies" from other terms in the agreement or from the agreement itself.[3] Such restraints upon the employer convert to another sort of job right for the employee.

On the procedural side, there are a number of what might be called "rights to remedies" which, insofar as they give the employee an extra hold on his job, may also legitimately be described as job rights. They include such features of the common-law employment relationship as the right to sue for wrongful discharge or on an implied promise by the employer of employment or continued employment. Although they obviously do not amount to substantive rights in the job, the existence of these remedies tends to protect employees against illicit separation from the job and, in the event of such separation, they provide damages. Thus they can be fairly described as job rights of still another sort.

There are thus numerous rights and remedies deriving from the common-law employment relationship which may properly be described as "job rights" (although not as "property rights"), and we shall examine them further. In addition to the traditional remedies which the common law provides for the redress of wrongs arising out of the employment relationship, the courts these days are increasingly hospitable to the idea of there being rights in the employment situation which were not deemed in earlier times to be there or which represent an enlargement of rights as they were earlier thought to be.

What we shall be discussing in the remainder of this chapter then, in the context of job rights, is the common-law employment contract, the common-law concept of "employment at will" (and how it is being modified to provide greater rights of redress for employees), and the common-law concept of "wrongful discharge" (also somewhat enlarged in modern times to provide the employee a greater access to a remedy). Our treatment of these subjects will necessarily be less than exhaustive for two principal reasons: (1) our purpose is only illustrative—to round out our catalog of job rights, real and potential, by highlighting other sources of such rights, and (2) much of the law relating to employment at will and wrongful discharge is concerned with *individual* grievances, and its relevance to our concerns (group dismissals in consequence of plant closings) is, therefore, limited.

2. Job Rights and the Employment Contract—"Employment at Will"

As one authority puts it, "Employment contracts of one form or another are as old as civilization itself."[4] A job, viewed separately from the work or task which it comprises, has been called a "contractual relationship" in that it consists of "a specification of the things that each party will (and must) do for the other in order for the relationship to continue."[5]

In its simplest form—the one which characterizes most factory employment transactions, for example—A hires B for a particular kind of work at a specified rate of pay and such other compensation and conditions as may be set forth in A's personnel policies or in the applicable union contract. Typically, the term of the employment is not fixed. It is indeterminate, terminable at the instance of either party. It is an "employment at will."[6]

At this point, what are the job rights of B and his fellow employees? In terms of tenure (which, in our plant-closing context, is our principal concern), *B,* according to the traditional view of the common law, could be terminated by *A* at any time for any cause which suited *A*—or no cause at all—just as *B* could quit whenever it pleased him to do so. That was the essence of common law employment at will.

But times change. There has always been a strong sense in American society of the importance of fair play. Accordingly, the ability of *A* to fire *B* capriciously has always made us uneasy and, today, is increasingly frowned upon. There is, in fact, a general societal aversion to action of any sort which is perceived as arbitrary or unreasonable or unfair (even though the pure *legal* right to take the action may be beyond question). In consequence, there has been a steady erosion of the at-will doctrine and a growing body of case law to the effect that employees' job rights (whatever may be) are safe from arbitrary or unreasonable extinction. The doctrines developed or expanded to achieve this result are found both in the law of contract and the law of tort.

3. *Wrongful Discharge, Implied Contracts, and "Good Faith and Fair Dealing"*

The law in this connection tends to be state law, rather than federal law, and it is both statutory and judge-made. Much of it need not concern us here, because it deals with abridgements of the at-will doctrine in the name of public policy, as by protecting "whistle-blowers'"[7] or by ordering the reinstatement of an employee discharged for refusing to commit perjury.[8]

Of somewhat more relevance to our inquiry are cases holding that personnel policy statements or employee handbooks may be used to make out an implied contract between employer and employee.[9] The *Touissant* case involved what the court found to be an implied commitment by the employer not to discharge without cause (a sort of express renunciation by the employer of his rights under common-law employment at will).

Indeed, what is known in the common law as the doctrine of implied contract could play a significant role in plant shutdown cases. That doctrine permits the court to "imply" the existence of a contract between the parties based on their behavior. The classic example is the case of a young man whose father promises him $1,000 if he refrains from smoking until he reaches his twenty-first birthday. In reliance on that promise, the young man gives up his right to smoke and, at age twenty-one, seeks to collect. His father resists, arguing that there was no contract between them, that the son made no promise and that, therefore, there was no consideration from the son to support the father's promise. Nonlawyer readers will be happy to learn that virtue is rewarded and welching is penalized by the common law in these circumstances. The rationale runs this way: there need be no express agreement, no handshake or writing, between the parties. The father made an offer which the son accepted, in the eyes of the law, by not smoking. The son, by giving up his right to smoke, incurred what the law (if not the Surgeon General) considers a detriment—he gave up a right in reliance on the promise—and the law implies a legally binding contract between them, for to do otherwise would be inequitable from the son's standpoint.

It takes no great imagination to extend this doctrine to a plant-closing situation where the employer gives employees assurances of continued employment in order to persuade them not to seek jobs elsewhere or not to quit in response to rumors that the plant is going to be shut down. The application of the "reliance to detriment" rationale in such a case is clear. We are about to see a case in which that was precisely the theory of the plaintiff's case.

There is another common-law doctrine which, though old, is equally contemporary. It, too, rests on the concept of fairness which, as we observed earlier, growingly pervades our society, especially in dealing with employment or other situations in which the power relationship is perceived as imbalanced. The doctrine that a "covenant of good faith and fair dealing" is an implied part of every contract is half a century old, at least, but it has been enjoying something of a revival. It holds that every contract contains an implied covenant that neither party will destroy or injure the right of the other to receive the benefits he contracted for,[10] as by frustrating performance of the contract or discharging an employee to prevent his collecting compensation earned under the contract.[11] Whether courts (which seem to be moving with some care into these new areas) will apply the covenant to an *implied* contract remains to be seen. If so, it would have the effect of greatly enlarging the job rights of employees who can bring themselves under this new and apparently expanding rubric.

We conclude by introducing a case that, one way or another, involves just about all of the principles which we have been discussing.

4. *The* Atari *Case*

This case involved a widely-publicized move in 1983 of the operations of the Atari Corporation, which manufactures video games and home computers, from the Santa Clara area of California to Hong Kong and Taiwan. Atari had been in serious difficulty for some time. Its problems (chiefly the related problems of costs and competition) had been developing for several years. By 1981, the company was seriously contemplating a move of its operations to the Far East, and its situation did not improve thereafter. For the year 1982, the company posted a loss in excess of $538 million.

There is some dispute as to what Atari's employees were told (and by whom) concerning the security of their jobs. At any rate, there appear to have been no mass defections, and there were still some six hundred employees on the Atari payroll on February 22, 1983, when they were abruptly informed that they were being terminated. The terminated employees were required to quit the plant on the same day, and they were instructed to pick up their final paychecks away from the plant, at a local high school.

Soon thereafter a class action suit on behalf of all the discharged employees was filed in California Superior Court by the Employment Law Center in San Francisco.[12] It named as defendants both Atari and its parent company, Warner Communications, together with various executive and supervisory personnel. The complaint alleged that, although Atari management had decided in 1981 or 1982 to move a substantial portion of its operations to the Far East, the plaintiffs were nevertheless systematically assured by various management personnel, as late as January 1983, that their jobs were secure. The complaint further stated that these assurances were authorized and that the employees "relied on these misrepresentations to their detriment."[13] The defendants were charged with, among other things, breach of contract, breach of the duty of good faith and fair dealing, and fraud.

The early responses of Atari to the complaint[14] argued, among other things, that the lawsuit was an "attempt to mount a challenge to the basic right of an employer to reduce the scope of its business and make consequent reductions in the size of its work force."[15]

Clearly, both sides view the *Atari* case as of major importance. The plaintiffs see it as an opportunity to modify the harsh rules of employment-at-will and to establish a set of employer duties or obligations toward employees (including notice) in a situation like Atari's. The defendants see it, as we have just noted, as a "challenge to the basic right of the employer" to change the scope of its business and to reduce its work force when business conditions require it.

In consequence of a good deal of preliminary legal skirmishing, the *Atari* case is still a long way from trial (if it ever goes to trial), and even further from a final decision. If and when the case is finally decided, however, it is likely to prove a landmark in the law of plant shutdown and job rights, particularly as we have been discussing them in this chapter. Because there was no employment contract or union agreement in the Atari situation, nor is there any plant-closing legislation in California, common-law job rights and remedies are a central feature of the case. The inclusion of a claim of "wrongful discharge" gives the *Atari* case an extra dimension. Until now, as we remarked earlier, the at-will and wrongful-discharge doctrines have been looked upon largely as an *individual,* rather than a collective, remedy.[16] The *Atari* case represents a clear attempt to apply those doctrines (in their modern liberalized form) to plant-closing situations.

It is not yet fully clear what defenses Atari will offer if the case goes to trial. Surely one will be that this was one of the situations in which the exigencies of the business precluded handling matters any differently. (It will be recalled that Justice Blackmun, in his opinion in *First National Maintenance Corporation,* referred to an employer's need, on occasion, for speed, flexibility, and secrecy.[17]) The company may also contend that the employees who remained in their jobs (or some of them, at least) did so in their own perceived interests, rather than "to their detriment" as alleged. The job market may have been unpromising, and the inclination may have been to stay with the job that was certain for as long as it might last. There is, in addition, the fact, well known to personnel executives, that employees (at all levels, from the lowest to the highest executive level) tend to defer acting upon bad news of this sort. If that phenomenon (or the job market situation earlier referred to) were at work in the *Atari* case, then it might be argued that any "assurances" given by management did not, in fact, affect the conduct of the employees at all—at least not in a manner which caused them to act "to their detriment."

Underlying all this, there is a deeper philosophical question. At least some job rights theorists proceed, as we saw in *Ozark Trailers,* on the theory that employees "invest" their labor in their jobs and, therefore, in the enterprise. If that rationale is accepted—if employees are to be deemed thus to be investors of their own human capital (a role which, in some respect, they cannot completely avoid in any event)—then it would seem that they cannot escape the investor's risk that when a business must fold for financial reasons it may not be able fully to compensate them for their investment.

Obviously, the *Atari* case will be well worth watching as it wends its way through the courts. It seems likely to make some new law in the job rights area—for example, as to the amount of advance notice an employer is required to give of a plant shutdown.[18] In addition, the plaintiffs no doubt hope to use the *Atari* case as a vehicle for infusing the common law with requirements of candor and fairness in dealing with employees in a shutdown situation. Such "fair play" for employees will, however, almost certainly carry an economic cost. Employers may find that they face an additional impediment to prompt action in response to market forces—an additional cost attached to the exercise of the traditional right of the owner of a business to deal with it as market conditions and his own judgment dictate. Whether such considerations will moderate judicial instincts to apply a compassionate "fix" to an admittedly difficult situation remains to be seen.

IX. Conclusion

In our Preface we pledged ourselves to the objective of "clarifying the terms of the public debate" on workers' rights and management rights in plant-closing situations. We hope that we have achieved that modest but useful goal.

In pursuit of it we analyzed the claims and the arguments, the statutes and the cases, and the common law of property, and we arrived at some definitions of "job rights" which we believe will prove useful. At the very least they ought to make possible a cooling of the rhetoric in which the debate in the future will be waged, for we found that a *literal* property (i.e., ownership) right in or to a job was not what most advocates of job rights are really seeking, whether they proceed by way of plant-closing legislation, or the National Labor Relations Act, or the common law. Indeed, it transpired that what most of us mean when we use the term "job rights" in closing situations is a set of claims against the employer, deriving, in one way or another and to one degree or another, from agreements, express or implied, in the course of establishing the employment relationship. Job rights properly understood, we conclude, deal with measures to mitigate for employees the economic pain attendant upon a plant shutdown.

We learned two things about job rights thus viewed: (1) there are far more job rights around, under existing law, than seem generally to have been supposed—that's the good news, but (2) the bad news—there is an economic cost attached to some job rights and it is not just the dollar cost of severance pay. It includes also the cost of legally imposed impediments to the deployment or redeployment of capital assets and the cost of delay in the execution or implementation of essential management decisions. These costs are real; they can be substantial; and they *will* be borne by *somebody,* both in the short term and in the long term. The candidates for bearing those costs (along with the costs associated with the process of severance and reemployment) are (1) the employees, (2) the enterprise, and (3) the society or the economy at large. Job rights advocates argue that part of these costs—the ones directly associated with the dislocation of employees—have fallen disproportionately on workers, and there have surely been cases where this has been true. They would, therefore, shift most or all of the cost to the employer or to the public by way of delaying—perhaps forestalling—the implementation of the plant-closing decision and loading it with additional costs through, *inter alia,* plant-closing legislation. To the extent that these shifts of costs are *mandated,* they are less desirable than solutions arrived at *voluntarily,* which can take account of the special circumstances of individual cases.

Workers cannot hope to escape entirely the effects of economic adversity which befalls the employer with whom they have chosen to cast their lot, but they are entitled (apart from whatever other actual rights they may have) to be treated humanely—with consideration and with fairness—in the severance process. Employers (if they intend to continue in business) have a corresponding stake in a reputation for ethical behavior, but they are necessarily limited by the available resources in what they can do in pursuit of that image. That is why it is counterproductive to try to mandate appropriate behavior by legislation or bureaucratic fiat. Commanding compassion or consideration by law, we keep having to learn, is no more feasible than mandating morality. Our system is contractarian and voluntary, and it works best when that fact is acknowledged.

It follows, we strongly suggest, that both employers and employees (and unions representing the latter) ought to *anticipate* the plant-closing situation, however remote that eventuality may seem, and deal with it. For employers without unions, this means adopting policies (which will become part of employment arrangements) that spell out rights and obligations and the procedures for implementing them in the event of a plant shutdown. For unionized operations, a similar forehandedness at the time of the negotiation of the union agreement is desirable, regardless of how remote a plant closing may seem. For some negotiators (on both sides) who have made an art form out of finessing hard questions and sweeping vexatious problems under the rug, this proposal will almost certainly be greeted with distaste—at first. Negotiators are urged, however, to ponder the advantages of addressing a problem *not* when the air is thick with shutdown panic and the drive for self-preservation is desperate, but rather in the cool atmosphere engendered by discussion of a problem which nobody thinks will arise. It is axiomatic that discussions are freer and more forthcoming, and concessions more readily made and accepted, when negotiations do not take place under the gun. Unions, in particular, will realize on reflection that (1) their traditional disinclination to engage in this sort of negotiation, which we noted earlier (p. 56, *ante*), may no longer serve their members' interests, and (2) they can negotiate more effectively when the climate is not one of crisis, at which time union bargaining leverage is apt to diminish rapidly.

Unions must be prepared to trade off "wages now" for "security then."[1] Management, for its part, must recognize that it will have to yield something in response, but much of what it will be asked to yield probably will be found to be in the area of fairness and equity in the *process,* which has no direct dollar cost and which need not unduly compromise essential flexibility and other managerial imperatives. For these and other reasons earlier assigned, the total package in a negotiation which addresses itself to the remote plant-closing possibility need not be excessively expensive.

In all cases, union and nonunion alike, we cannot stress too strongly the virtues of candor and collaboration. Consultation (when not mandatory—and sometimes even when it is) *can* produce solutions and, if we read trends in employee relations correctly, this is the wave of the future. Perhaps its most important virtue, aside from the fact that it tends to yield tailor-made solutions, is that it tends also to dispense altogether with the vocabulary of rights.

NOTES

Chapter I

1. It is worth observing here that notwithstanding a rather general notion that we are a highly mobile society, actually we are not—at least, not at the blue-collar level. Roots are strong and change is threatening. The constituency for barriers against plant closings is, therefore, large.

2. *See, passim,* Studs Terkel's *Hard Times* (New York: Pantheon Books, 1970). Whether different notions (and possibly less compassion) should apply in the case of persons whose economic misfortunes were *not* (or not entirely) the result of circumstances beyond their control—where, for example, economic adversity could be traced to overachievement at the bargaining table and subsequent and consequent disemployment—is a question not frequently raised.

3. A sample: "Most of these [proposed legislative] solutions are aimed at preventing joblessness, not at encouraging business survival or creating a climate that encourages new business and generates new jobs." Jerry J. Jasinowski, chief economist for the National Association of Manufacturers, writing in the *Christian Science Monitor* ("When Plants Close"), August 13, 1985, at 17.

4. *Christian Science Monitor,* August 13, 1985, *supra.*

5. Another executive arm, the United States Department of Labor, recently appointed a task force to study the problem.

Chapter II

1. Since most of the efforts at the state level have been unsuccessful thus far, no useful purpose would be served by a detailed analysis here of the proposed laws, although it is of some interest to identify who supports such legislation and why, and what its effects are likely to be, and that will be done. Readers interested in the details of plant-closing laws at the state level, as well as in an excellent statement of the case against them, are urged to see R. McKenzie, *Fugitive Industry: The Economics and Politics of Deindustrialization* (San Francisco: Pacific Institute for Public Policy Research, 1984).

2. *See* McKenzie, *op. cit. supra,* xxi *et seq.,* Foreword by Professor Welch. Professor Welch's Foreword also provides an excellent statement of the case for capital mobility, as well as the economic case against plant-closing restrictions in general.

3. *See,* e.g., National Employment Priorities Act of 1983, H.R. 2847, 96th Cong., 1st Sess., containing the features common to all the state plant-closing proposals: notice, severance pay, and "restitution" payments to the community.

4. Congressman Ford was somewhat more explicit in the article which he wrote for the *Labor Law Journal* soon after introducing his bill. He describes it as "more politically viable" than his earlier efforts, a description that is somewhat puzzling in light of the following statement of his objectives:

> It is time for everyone to realize that the managers of American business do not always know what is best for their own firms, much less what is best for their employees and their communities. There is far too much at stake to let disinvestment decisions be made in distant corporate boardrooms without any input from those whose lives will be most directly affected. W. Ford, *Coping with Plant Closings,* 36 Labor L. J. 323, 325 (1985).

It may be that his frankly antimanagement objectives helped to defeat Mr. Ford's bill.

5. An interesting aspect of the Ford bill was that while the *notice* requirements were applied not only to unionized employees but also to nonunionized employees, the *consultation* (i.e., bargaining) provisions were confined to employees represented by a union, and the principal thrust of the bill was in the direction of providing protection and remedies for unionized employees only. In this respect, the Ford bill differs markedly from the state proposals, which tend to make no distinction between unionized and nonunionized employees and to cover all employees alike.

6. Section 8(d) of the Act describes the duty to bargain collectively as the duty to "meet and confer in good faith."

7. The House deleted this provision, presumably, because it was a special focus of opposition, but Mr. Ford's bill still went down to defeat, despite other attempts to water it down to an acceptable level.

8. It will be recalled that "employment loss" was defined in terms of dislocation, rather than wage loss, so Congressman Ford evidently had in mind making the employer pay damages irrespective of any direct monetary loss in terms of wages. The object of *deterring* plant closings was quite plain here and elsewhere in the Ford bill.

9. The case for this sort of solution to the plant-closing problem is eloquently put in Bluestone and Harrison, *The Deindustrialization of America: Plant Closings, Community Abandonment, and the Dismantling of Basic Industry* (New York: Basic Books, 1982).

10. McKenzie, *op. cit. supra,* Preface at xxvi.

11. *See* McKenzie and Yandle, *Plant Closing Laws: Their Union Support* in *J. of Lab. Research* (Winter, 1981).

12. *See* McKenzie, *Fugitive Industry, op. cit. supra,* at 7.

13. *Id.,* Preface at xxv-xxvi.

Chapter III

1. National Labor Relations Act, as amended [principally by the Labor-Management Relations (Taft-Hartley) Act of 1947], 29 *U.S.C.* § 151 *et seq.* (1982). For the convenience of the reader, subsequent citations to the Act will accord with the popular practice of referring only to the specific sections of the Act itself.

2. The remainder of section 8(a)(3) deals with the union shop as an exception to the prohibition against "encouraging membership."

3. *See* National Lawyers Guild, *Plant Closings and Runaway Industries: Strategies for Labor* (Washington: National Labor Law Center, 1981) at 5.

4. Should such charges be accepted and prosecuted by the National Labor Relations Board, the very fact of the proceeding can have a positive effect among the employees whom the union is seeking to organize.

5. *See, passim,* C. Morris, *The Developing Labor Law* (Washington: Bureau of National Affairs, 2d ed., 1983), Ch. 7.

6. Darlington Mfg. Co., 139 N.L.R.B. 241, 51 L.R.R.M. 1278 (1962), *enf. denied sub nom.* Darlington Mfg. Co. v. NLRB, 325 F. 2d 682 (4th Cir. 1963), *rev'd. sub nom.* Textile Workers v. Darlington Mfg. Co., 380 U.S. 253 (1965).

7. The refusal to bargain charge was never the significant issue in the *Darlington* case, and it ultimately disappeared for all practical purposes.

8. 325 F. 2d at 685.

9. 380 U.S. at 268.

10. 380 U.S. at 274.

11. To nobody's surprise, the NLRB found, on the remand, that both criteria were satisfied on the facts of the *Darlington* case, and it accordingly ordered the company to provide back pay to its terminated employees, until such time as they either found other employment or had been placed on a preferential hiring list by Deering-Milliken for its other operations.

12. 380 U.S. at 270.

13. It is a common misapprehension to believe that collective bargaining was somehow a creature of the New Deal. It was not. What was newly introduced at that time was the *compulsory* feature of collective bargaining. Voluntary collective bargaining had been practiced for many years in a variety of industries, such as construction, coal mining, and railroads. Indeed, the Railway Labor Act of 1926 was something of a precursor, in terms of labor legislation, of the Wagner Act of 1935. It did not *impose* the duty to bargain, however. Bargaining was already being practiced, and it simply built upon that foundation. By making collective bargaining compulsory in the Wagner Act, Congress not only dramatically abridged what employers saw as their traditional and inherent right to manage the enterprise, but it injected employees and their unions into the management decision-making process, first as to wages, hours, and other conditions of employment, and later into management decisions affecting jobs, and thus, ultimately, into plant-closing decisions.

14. The Act, as amended in 1947, also imposes a duty to bargain on unions and hence the two-sided language of section 8(d), quoted below, but we are not concerned here with the *union's* duty to bargain.

15. *See* the historical references collected in O'Connell, "Collective Bargaining and the Rule of Law" in *Collective Bargaining: Survival in the 70's* (Rowen, ed.) (Philadelphia: University of Pennsylvania, 1972) at 101 n. 1.

16. *See* C. Morris, *op. cit. supra,* note 5, at 758.

17. One recent commentator noted "the almost continuous attempts of the National Labor Relations Board, and particularly its General Counsel, to expand NLRB authority over managerial actions in the name of promoting collective bargaining." Miscimarra, *The NLRB and Managerial Discretion* (Philadelphia: The Wharton School, Labor Relations and Public Policy Series No. 24, 1983) at iii.

Chapter IV

1. Fibreboard Paper Products Corp. v. NLRB, 379 U.S. 203 (1964).

2. *See,* for example (*infra,* page 63 *et seq.*), our discussion of the instructions issued by the general counsel of the Board following the unfavorable (to the Board) decision of the United States Supreme Court in the *First National Maintenance* case.

3. Fibreboard Paper Products Corp., 130 N.L.R.B. 1558, 47 L.R.R.M. 1547 (1961). As we shall see, the case was before the Board twice and its decisions have come to be known, respectively, as *Fibreboard I* and *Fibreboard II.*

4. 130 N.L.R.B. at 1568. (Quoted in Intermediate Report of Administrative Law Judge, not reprinted in L.R.R.M.)

5. 130 N.L.R.B. at 1561, 47 L.R.R.M. at 1549.

6. Town & Country Mfg. Co., 136 N.L.R.B. 1022, 49 L.R.R.M. 1918 (1962), *enforced* Town & Country Mfg. Co. v. NLRB, 316 F. 2d 846 (5th Cir. 1963).

7. 136 N.L.R.B. at 1027, 49 L.R.R.M. at 1920. The Board's decision, although not attributed as is the custom, was, in fact, written by Member (later Chairman) John Fanning, concerning whose views we shall have more to say later. The Board would later withdraw its assurance to management that the new bargaining obligation "in nowise restrains an employer from formulating or effectuating an economic decision to terminate a phase of his business operations." Although the *Town & Country* case involved an antiunion animus feature, like *Darlington,* the Board chose not to place its reliance on that factor. Instead, determined to establish the doctrine of decision bargaining, it held squarely that "the elimination of unit jobs, albeit for economic reasons, is a matter within the statutory phrase 'other terms and conditions of employment' and is a mandatory subject of collective bargaining." *Ibid.*

8. Fibreboard Paper Products Corp., 138 N.L.R.B. 550, 51 L.R.R.M. 1101 (1962).

9. 138 N.L.R.B. at 559-60, 51 L.R.R.M. at 1103. Emphasis added.

10. 138 N.L.R.B. at 560, 51 L.R.R.M. at 1103-04.

11. Fibreboard Paper Products Corp. v. NLRB, 379 U.S. 203 (1964).

12. East Bay Union of Machinists, Local 1304 United Steelworkers of America v. NLRB, 322 F. 2d 411 (D.C. Cir. 1963).

13. Until *Fibreboard,* reinstatement and back pay were generally considered to be remedies for discriminatory discharge, although the Act, in empowering the Board to impose those remedies, does not so confine them.

14. 379 U.S. at 209.

15. 379 U.S. at 210.

16. For example, in one of the opinion's key sentences, the chief justice says that the Court is "not expanding the scope of mandatory bargaining" by its holding, which he thereupon describes as being that "the type of 'contracting out' involved in this case [substitution of one set of employees for another] is a statutory subject of collective bargaining under section 8(d)." 379 U.S. at 214. But the issue which made the case so important, of course, had not so much to do with the *type* of management action, as with the bargainability of the managerial *decision* to take that type of action.

17. 379 U.S. at 214.

18. 379 U.S. at 217. That the Stewart opinion is a *concurring,* not a dissenting, opinion is of considerable importance. His views explain and define the principal opinion, while concurring in its conclusion, and thus the chief justice's opinion must be read *with* Justice Stewart's opinion to gain an appreciation of what the Court, *as a whole,* held in *Fibreboard* and (perhaps more importantly) what it did not hold.

19. 379 U.S. at 218.

20. 379 U.S. at 222-23. It is arguable that Justice Stewart gave up too easily the issue of whether or not the existence of a job can properly be deemed a "condition of employment" for purposes of the statutory obligation to bargain. The employer's duty to bargain, after all, extends only to the "representatives of his employees." If there are no employees, the duty to bargain loses its basis. The decision not to *continue* operations (and, therefore, the decision no longer to employ anybody in those operations) is not, it would seem, different in principle from a decision to *start* an operation and to employ people for that operation. Except in the construction industry, for which the Act makes an explicit and complicated allowance in favor of "pre-hire agreements" with construction unions, there is no authority (nor does it seem that there could logically be any) for the proposition that an entrepreneur considering the starting of a business must bargain with some union over whether he shall do so and, if he decides to go ahead, over whom he shall employ. That logic, we suggest, might be applied equally to the exit decision. In that connection, we are not aware that theatrical unions, for example, have ever insisted upon being bargained with over the decision to close a failing show. The reasons which have persuaded them not to urge such a right are, of course, the same as those which apply to any other economically pressed operation. We mention this point concerning the bargainability of the question of whether or not a job shall exist because, being critical to the area of the law which we are examining, it is worthy of more extended consideration than it seems to have received. Another related point which likewise deserves a closer and more challenging look is the Board's interpretation of the bargaining duty imposed by the Act as applying not only to wages, hours, etc., but also to any action which might *affect* those things (which is a very different and much broader concept and is, of course, the foundation for holding that there is a duty to bargain over a shutdown).

21. 379 U.S. at 223.

22. *Ibid.*

23. 379 U.S. at 225.

24. Adams Dairy, Inc., 137 N.L.R.B. 815, 50 L.R.R.M. 1281 (1962).

25. NLRB v. Adams Dairy, Inc., 322 F. 2d 553 (8th Cir. 1963). In addition to holding that the company's decision "to terminate a phase of its business and distribute all of its products through independent contractors was not a required subject of collective bargaining" (322 F. 2d at 562), the Court laid stress on the company's lack of antiunion animus—absence of an intent to commit an unfair labor practice. Curiously, the absence of antiunion animus appears to influence the courts more than the Board; the Board increasingly appears, as the cases unfold, to find the *presence* of antiunion animus of overriding significance, but its *absence* unimportant. This inconsistency has made no contribution to clarity in the law.

26. NLRB v. Adams Dairy, Inc., 379 U.S. 644 (1965).

27. NLRB v. Adams Dairy, Inc., 350 F. 2d 103 (8th Cir. 1965).

28. Wm. J. Burns Int'l Detective Agency, 346 F. 2d 897 (8th Cir. 1965).

29. Wm. J. Burns Int'l Detective Agency, 148 N.L.R.B. 1267, 57 L.R.R.M. 1163 (1964).

30. 346 F. 2d at 901. The court seems to have overlooked (and the Board ignored) the fact that the Creighton contract termination was, by its nature, neither entirely internal nor unilateral on Burns's part. The decision to terminate services was made by the University. The subsequent action by Burns simply acknowledged that fact and was, in that sense, purely a business decision in which, it would seem, collective bargaining could play no role. In a similar situation (*First National Maintenance*) discussed in Chapter V, the Supreme Court refused to enforce a decision-bargaining order.

31. 346 F. 2d at 902.

32. Chapter III, *ante*, note 9, and accompanying text.

33. Morrison Cafeterias Consol., Inc. v. NLRB, 431 F. 2d 254 (8th Cir. 1970).

34. Morrison Cafeterias Consol., Inc., 148 N.L.R.B. 139, 56 L.R.R.M. 1483 (1964).

35. 177 N.L.R.B. at 591, 596, 71 L.R.R.M. at 1449 (1969). ALJ decision not reprinted in L.R.R.M.

36. 431 F. 2d at 256. The relevant portion of Member Zagoria's dissent reads as follows:

> The Supreme Court's ruling in *Darlington* completely foreclosed finding an unlawful refusal to bargain in the instant case, either as to the decision to close or as to the effects of that decision. A finding of an 8(a)(5) violation under *Darlington* depends entirely upon a finding of an 8(a)(3) violation. *Hence, the partial closing of a business, like the complete cessation of a business, cannot be found to constitute a violation of section 8(a)(5) in the absence of motivation aimed at achieving the prohibited effect, that is, to chill unionism in other parts of the enterprise.* In other words, as I read the Supreme Court's decision in *Darlington*, as long as it is not for the purpose of chilling unionism among his remaining employees, an employer may close part of his business "for any reason he pleases." (Emphasis added.) *Quoted at* 431 F. 2d at 257.

37. *Ibid.*

38. NLRB v. Royal Plating & Polishing Co., 350 F. 2d 191 (3rd Cir. 1965).

39. NLRB v. Transmarine Navigation Corp., 380 F. 2d 933 (9th Cir. 1967).

40. NLRB v. Thompson Transport Co., 406 F. 2d 698 (10th Cir. 1969).

41. Ozark Trailers, Inc., 161 N.L.R.B. 561, 63 L.R.R.M. 1264 (1966).

42. Perhaps Ozark could not afford the cost of an appeal (a significant factor in these situations) or it may not have been worth the cost, since the Board did not require the shut plant to be reopened or the employees reinstated, but only that back pay be paid for the limited period between the time the decision was made and the date when the plant was actually closed. In any case, *Ozark Trailers* (and the workers' rights theory which, as we are about to see, it expounds) was not passed on by any appellate court.

43. 161 N.L.R.B. at 566, 63 L.R.R.M. at 1267.

44. *See* note 48, *infra*, and Chapter VI, note 15, and accompanying text.

45. *See* Milwaukee Spring Div. of Ill. Coil Spring, 265 N.L.R.B. 206, 181 L.R.R.M. 1486 (1982), discussed in Chapter VI, *post*.

46. *See* O'Connell, "The Implications of Decision Bargaining" in *New York University Conference on Labor*, Vol. 16 (Washington: Bureau of National Affairs, 1963).

47. 161 N.L.R.B. at 569, 63 L.R.R.M. at 1269.

48. The Board here was displaying not so much a bias *against* management as simple ignorance of the realities of day-to-day operations—a flaw which it repeatedly demonstrates.

49. The composition and philosophy of the Board have been undergoing significant change as the result of appointments made to the Board by President Reagan. *See* Chapter VII, *post*, and compare the similar situation under President Kennedy, notes 6 and 7, *supra*, and accompanying text.

50. 191 N.L.R.B. at 951, 73 L.R.R.M. at 1538 (1971).

51. One of the dissenters was Member (later Chairman) Fanning who, as we have noted, was the author of the decision-bargaining doctrine.

52. 191 N.L.R.B. at 951, 73 L.R.R.M. at 1539.

53. 191 N.L.R.B. at 952, 73 L.R.R.M. at 1539.

54. As we shall see, a debate subsequently developed over "amenability" with proponents of decision bargaining arguing that if the subject of a management decision was at all susceptible of being bargained about, then that was a sufficient reason for imposing mandatory bargaining. Others (including the Supreme Court) took a more restrained view of the nature and role of amenability.

55. *Ibid.*

56. Summit Tooling Co. and Ace Tool Engineering Co., 195 N.L.R.B. 479, 79 L.R.R.M. 1396 (1972).

57. Chairman Miller did not sit on this case. It was decided by a panel composed of Members Fanning and Howard Jenkins (another holdover) and Member Ralph Kennedy, a Nixon appointee.

58. 195 N.L.R.B. at 480, 79 L.R.R.M. at 1400.

59. 195 N.L.R.B. at 481, 79 L.R.R.M. at 1401. Briefly stated, this involved providing that the discharged employees would continue to receive back pay until the bargaining resulted in agreement or impasse or the union failed to follow up on the bargaining order. We shall encounter this remedy again.

60. *See* St. Louis Coca Cola Bottling Co., 188 N.L.R.B. 658, 76 L.R.R.M. 1599 (1971); Fraser & Johnston Co., 189 N.L.R.B. 142, 77 L.R.R.M. 1036 (1971); R. L. Sweet Lumber Co., 207 N.L.R.B. 529, 85 L.R.R.M. 1073 (1973). *Cf.* Los Angeles Marine Hardware Co., 235 N.L.R.B. 720, 98 L.R.R.M. 1571 (1978) and Milwaukee Spring Div. of Ill. Coil Spring Co., 265 N.L.R.B. 206, 181 L.R.R.M. 1486 (1982), both discussed in detail in Chapter VI, *post.*

Chapter V

1. First Nat'l Maintenance Corp. v. NLRB, 452 U.S. 666 (1981). Except as otherwise indicated, our statement of the facts is derived from the opinion of the Supreme Court.

2. First Nat'l Maintenance Corp., 242 N.L.R.B. 462, 101 L.R.R.M. 1177 (1979).

3. *Id.* at 465 L.R.R.M. does not contain the text of the ALJ decision.

4. *Id.* at 466.

5. *Id.* at 463, 466, 101 L.R.R.M. at 1178-79.

6. First Nat'l Maintenance Corp. v. NLRB, 627 F. 2d 569, 601 (2d Cir. 1980).

7. *Id.* at 601.

8. 452 U.S. at 672-73, citing, *inter alia,* the *Adams Dairy, Transmarine Navigation,* and *Thompson Transport* decisions to which we referred in Chapter IV, *ante.*

9. *Id.* at 673, citing the decisions in *Burns* and *Morrison Cafeterias* discussed in Chapter IV.

10. *Id.* at 674.

11. *Id.* at 667.

12. *Id.* at 676, citing and quoting from Chemical & Alkali Workers v. Pittsburgh Plate Glass Co., 404 U.S. 157, 178 (1971).

13. 452 U.S. at 677.

14. *Ibid.*, quoting Justice Stewart's similar language (*see* pages 34-35, *supra*) concerning management decisions which are not "primarily about conditions of employment," even though "the effect of the decision may necessarily be to terminate employment."

15. 452 U.S. at 684.

16. 452 U.S. at 678-79.

17. 452 U.S. at 667.

18. *Ibid.*

19. *Id.*, note 15. *See also* NLRB v. First Nat'l Maintenance Corp., 627 F. 2d 596, 598.

20. 452 U.S. at 677. Although possibly unaware that it is venturing on terrain which is somewhat controversial among labor lawyers, the Court majority is here relying on the theory of management's inherent rights (or "retained freedom," as the opinion puts it). This is the theory that there are rights pertinent to the operation of an enterprise which inhere in the ownership/management of the enterprise and are not affected by the intervention of a union, unless they are abridged by the provisions of a union contract (there were none in *FNM*). We discuss this further in Chapter VII.

21. 452 U.S. at 678.

22. 452 U.S. at 679.

23. 452 U.S. at 680.

24. 452 U.S. at 681.

25. 452 U.S. at 683.

26. 452 U.S. at 681.

27. It could not have been done by the union here, because, as we noted in our summary of the facts, no contract negotiations ever took place. It is important to bear this fact (which distinguishes *FNM* from most other plant-closing cases) in mind as we follow the Court's reasoning.

28. 452 U.S. at 683.

29. 452 U.S. at 684-85.

30. 452 U.S. at 686.

31. We suggest, in passing, that although Justice Blackmun does not discuss or cite the *Darlington* case at this point, he has nevertheless arrived at the same conclusion that we suggest in our analysis of that case (*see* section 3, *infra*, at 61): *Darlington* implicitly holds that a complete shutdown of one plant out of a several-plant operation is as free of the Act as is the *total* (going-out-of-business) shutdown, when the reasons for the partial shutdown "focus," as Justice Blackmun put it, on the economics of the business rather than on its "employment relationship" aspects (although they will also be present), and when there is no question of any antiunion animus.

32. Having provided a practical framework for determining whether in a given case a decision-bargaining duty is imposed by the Act, and having decided pursuant to the principles it expounded that FNM had no duty to bargain over its decision, the Court abruptly dropped a footnote (452 U.S. at 686 n. 22) which has given rise to some debate. Its purpose is the familiar one of disclaiming that the Court was deciding cases not before it. The footnote reads as follows: "In this opinion we of course intimate no view as to other types of management decisions, such as plant relocations, sales, other kinds of subcontracting, automation, etc., which are to be considered on their particular facts."

As we shall see, some have taken that language as having the effect of narrowly confining the case to its special facts. We suggest a different view. For one thing, it is not at all uncommon for the Court to assert that it is not deciding anything but the case before it. That is appropriate judicial behavior and allows subsequent courts to reach different conclusions on different facts without constraint. That, however, is far from asserting that the Court was not engaged in this case in laying down principles of general application. As we noted at the outset, the Court seemed bent on trying to settle the law. Footnote 22 is not inconsistent with that objective. It mentions, by way of example, four other types of cases in which management decisions might be argued to be subject to mandatory decision bargaining. Two of them (subcontracting, plant relocations) might very well involve, as *Fibreboard* did, factual situations that would permit the Court to find the balance (unlike the case before it) weighted in favor of mandatory decision bargaining. The considerations that would lead it to do so are fully explored in *First National Maintenance*. The other two (sales and automation), on the other hand, seem unlikely to involve factual situations in which mandatory decision bargaining would be appropriate: the employment effect of the managerial decision might be (in the Court's own language) merely "indirect and attenuated," or the subject matter of the decision might not be "amenable" to the bargaining process—either because it was unsuited to negotiation or because there was no possibility that the union could contribute to a solution of the management problem—or the business exigencies might be "sufficiently compelling to obviate the duty to bargain." Thus the Court's examples themselves show the need for, and the application of, the very rules and criteria which the Court laid down in the *FNM* case.

Why, then, did the Court append the limiting language? We have already suggested one answer: judicial propriety and custom. Another is that Justice Blackmun may have found it necessary to include footnote 22 in order to command a majority in support of the remainder of his views. In any case, the phrase was, not surprisingly, exploited by the Board and its general counsel (*see* section 4, *infra*) in an effort to mitigate the significance of the *First National Maintenance* decision and to evade its impact on the decisional policy which the Board was intent on pursuing.

33. 452 U.S. at 687-88.

34. *Ibid.*

35. *Ibid.*

36. Note that the foregoing criteria apply only to decision bargaining; effects bargaining, as indicated earlier, is widely accepted as appropriate in nearly every situation, with the exception of those in which no bargaining at all is required (e.g., a total shutdown or where the union has waived by contract its right to bargain). *See also* our discussion in Chapter VII of effects bargaining in connection with the dissenting opinion in the *Otis Elevator* case.

37. *See* Chapter IV, note 36, and accompanying text.

38. *See*, for example, Note, *Enforcing the NLRA: The Need for a Duty to Bargain over Partial Plant Closings,* 60 Texas L. Rev. 279 (1982).

39. General Counsel Lubbers was appointed by President Carter just before the latter left office. Consequently, Mr. Lubbers served most of his term under President Reagan. Ultimately, this was the source of some embarrassment. Usually, the general counsel and the majority of the Board he serves are philosophically eye-to-eye. That was true of Mr. Lubbers and the Board majority at the time when the Supreme Court handed down its decision in *First National Maintenance*. By the end of his term, however, Mr. Lubbers found himself in deep disagreement with the philosophy of the Board that he was by then serving, a majority of whom had been appointed by President Reagan. We shall later be seeing some of the results of this unusually sharp conflict.

40. Office of the General Counsel, Memorandum 81-57, November 30, 1981, *Daily Labor Report* No. 10 (January 15, 1982), § E.

41. For a comprehensive treatment of injunctions under section 10(j) of the Act, insofar as they may be employed in plant relocation situations, *see* Rogalski, *The Propriety of Issuing an Injunction to Prevent a Plant From Relocating Under Section 10(j) of the National Labor Relations Act,* 78 N.W. U.L. Rev. 673 (1983).

42. D.L.R. No. 10, *supra,* at E-1.

43. In his preoccupation with evading *First National Maintenance,* Mr. Lubbers seems not to have noticed that he might be backing into *Darlington.* As we noted earlier, that case was strong on proprietary rights in the going-out-of-business situation where (as in *FNM*) there was no antiunion animus.

44. D.L.R. No. 10 at E-1. Emphasis in original.

45. John Irving, himself a former general counsel of the Board, in a scathing commentary on the Lubbers "Guidelines." *Daily Labor Report* No. 17 (January 26, 1982), § D, at D-4.

46. *See* note 32, *supra.*

47. "Bargaining...should be required only if the benefit, for labor-management relations and the collective bargaining process, outweighs the burden placed on the business." First Nat'l Maintenance Corp. v. NLRB, *supra,* 452 U.S. 679.

48. Actually, he rather stands it on end: "If the factors which indicate that the decision is amenable to the process of collective bargaining clearly outweigh the factors which indicate that bargaining would be burdensome," the employer who fails or refuses to bargain has, Mr. Lubbers instructs the staff, violated the Act, and a proceeding should commence against him. What Lubbers did, in effect, was to equate amenability with "benefit" —something the Court quite pointedly did not do—and thus the test framed by Mr. Lubbers (which might be colloquially framed as "if it *can* be bargained about, it *must* be bargained about") would, it would seem, nearly always result in the imposition of a bargaining duty by the Board. This, of course, was Mr. Lubbers's intent. It was not the Supreme Court's.

49. D.L.R. No. 10, *supra,* at D-2.

Chapter VI

1. Milwaukee Spring Div. of Ill. Coil Spring Co., 265 N.L.R.B. 206, 111 L.R.R.M. 1486 (1982).

2. Concession bargaining (or "give-backs," to use a union term) is the name given to a negotiation looking towards some relief for the employer from terms (usually wages or benefits *in futuro*) previously agreed upon with the union and embodied in a union contract.

3. The parties stipulated, among other things, that the four entities were "a single employing enterprise." The stipulation aspect of the case is important, for it meant that unlike the vast majority of litigated Board cases, there was in *Milwaukee Spring* no dispute over the facts. They were, on the contrary, agreed upon by the employer, the union, and the general counsel of the Board. In consequence, there was no trial, and the case went to the Board for decision, insofar as the facts were concerned, on the basis of the parties' stipulation.

4. The case does not disclose what these other concessions were, but it can be speculated that they dealt with work practices or other nonwage terms of the union contract which contribute to labor costs.

5. The actual figures were: At Milwaukee Spring, average hourly rates of $8.00 and fringe costs of $2.00 (a total of $10.00 per hour), while at McHenry (the proposed relocation site), the same costs were $4.50 and $1.35 respectively (for a total of $5.85 per hour), a differential of $4.15—or over 40 percent—in wage costs alone.

6. 265 N.L.R.B. at 207, 111 L.R.R.M. at 1487. Quoted material is from the Board's decision and, presumably, is either quoted from, or is a paraphrase of, the above-mentioned stipulation of facts.

7. *Ibid.*

8. It is worth remarking in passing that, although the Board seemed unaware of it, it is by no means uncommon for union contracts to contain a "work jurisdiction" clause by which the employer agrees, in one way or another, that the union and its members do have a "right to the work." For the Board to arbitrarily read such a provision into a contract, when it has not been negotiated into it, is not only to ignore the canons of labor relations practice, but it would seem to be a significant interference with the principle of free and voluntary collective bargaining.

9. *See, ante,* the discussion of the *Ozark Trailers* case (Chapter IV, Section 3).

10. Milwaukee Spring Div., 265 N.L.R.B. 209, 111 L.R.R.M. 1489.

11. *Ibid.* The Board relied on Los Angeles Marine Hardware Co., 235 N.L.R.B. 720, 98 L.R.R.M. 1571 (1978), but it appears to have misread that case. In *Los Angeles Marine* (more fully discussed below), the geographical description appeared *only* in the so-called preamble and *not* (as in *Milwaukee Spring*) in the recognition clause as well, and the decision in *Los Angeles Marine* made a point of that fact: "In fact, the language appears in the preamble in connection with a description of the parties to the agreement and is not restated in the portion of the agreement which described the bargaining unit i.e., the recognition clause." 235 N.L.R.B. at 736. (Full text of decision not reprinted in L.R.R.M.) In *Milwaukee Spring,* the language appears in *both* places—the preamble and the recognition clause—and one of the main functions of the recognition clause, as we have noted above, is to define the extent of the coverage of the union agreement.

12. 265 N.L.R.B. at 209-10, 111 L.R.R.M. at 1489.

13. *Id.* at 210, 111 L.R.R.M. at 1489. Emphasis added.

14. *See* § 4, *infra.*

15. *See* O'Connell, "Trends in Labor Law" in *Collective Bargaining Today* (Washington: BNA, 1971) at 206, 212-13. *See also* Miscimarra, *op. cit. supra,* Chapter III, note 17, at 207.

16. *See* §§ 3 and 4, *infra.*

17. 265 N.L.R.B. at 208, 210, 111 L.R.R.M. at 1488-89, 1490. The use to which the Board seeks to put the "inherently destructive" concept (i.e., to make out a sort of *per se* violation of section 8(a)(3)) seems strikingly inappropriate in light of the stipulation by all of the parties that the employer did not entertain any antiunion animus—an essential ingredient of a violation of section 8(a)(3). Thus the Board, by a sort of presumption of law, was importing into the case an element which the parties expressly agreed was not present. The injection of the same rationale into *Los Angeles Marine, infra,* was only slightly less inappropriate. *See* Miscimarra, *op. cit. supra,* Chapter III, note 17, at 210.

18. *See* Chapter V, Section 4, *ante.*

19. 265 N.L.R.B. at 209 n. 4, 111 L.R.R.M. at 1488 n. 4.

20. Milwaukee Spring Div. of Ill. Coil Spring Co. v. NLRB, 718 F. 2d 1102 (7th Cir. 1983).

21. Discussed in Section 2 of Chapter VII, *post*.

22. The reader will note the historical resemblance to the earlier handling by the Board of the equally controversial *Fibreboard* decision during the Kennedy Administration recounted in Chapter IV, Section 1.

23. Miscimarra, *op cit. supra,* Chapter III, note 17, at 204.

24. Los Angeles Marine Hardware Co., a Division of Mission Marine Associates, Inc., 235 N.L.R.B. 720, 98 L.R.R.M. 1571 (1978).

25. *Id*. at 732-33. Text of ALJ decision not reprinted in L.R.R.M.

26. *Id*. at 735. The Board's order in *Los Angeles Marine* was enforced a year later, almost perfunctorily, by the U.S. Court of Appeals. Los Angeles Marine Hardware Co. v. NLRB, 602 F. 2d 1302 (9th Cir. 1979).

27. *Id*. at 737.

28. *Id*. at 735.

29. "It is universally recognized and accepted that a collective bargaining agreement does not guarantee employment for the life of the agreement, absent a clear and explicit contract provision to the contrary." Miscimarra, *op. cit. supra,* Chapter III, note 17, at 208 n. 82.

30. It is worth remarking, in conclusion, that had the rationale of Chairman Fanning and his colleagues on the Carter Board survived, it would have constituted a giant step toward the creation of a genuine "right-to-the-job," indefeasible by unilateral action of the employer and enforceable under the Act—a truly radical development in American labor-management affairs.

31. Were Mr. Lubbers and the Carter Board still in office, this document would merit the closest scrutiny. It is truly remarkable for its bold disregard of traditional notions concerning management rights, the meaning of common terms found in ordinary union contracts, and the (theretofore) accepted interpretation of the Act. As it is, we shall deal with it only to the extent necessary to indicate its flavor, as a matter of historical interest, and to provide the grounding necessary to make meaningful certain aspects of the revisionary decision of the Reagan Board in *Milwaukee Spring II*.

32. Quarterly Report of N.L.R.B. General Counsel William A. Lubbers, *Daily Labor Report* No. 3 (January 5, 1983), Section D (Washington: BNA, 1983) at D-1.

33. Note 29, *supra,* and accompanying text.

34. D.L.R., January 5, 1983, *supra,* at D-1, citing *Los Angeles Marine*.

35. *Id*. at D-1.

36. *Id*. at D-2 and 3. Both local unions were members of the same international union.

Chapter VII

1. Opinion is not unanimous on this score. Some feel that it is entirely appropriate for an administrative agency like the Board to reflect the election returns and the political philosophy of a new president. For a thoughtful review of both sides, *see* Bierman, *Reflections on the Problem of Labor Board Instability,* 62 Denver L. Rev. 551 (1985).

2. Milwaukee Spring Div. of Ill. Coil Spring Co., 268 N.L.R.B. 601, 115 L.R.R.M. 1065 (1984).

3. Milwaukee Spring Div. of Ill. Coil Spring Co. v. NLRB, 718 F. 2d 1102 (7th Cir. 1983), without opinion.

4. 268 N.L.R.B. at 602, 115 L.R.R.M. at 1066.

5. Ibid.

6. See Chapter V, note 20, and accompanying text.

7. 268 N.L.R.B. at 602, 115 L.R.R.M. at 1067.

8. Ibid., citing Boeing Co. v. NLRB, 581 F. 2d 793, 99 L.R.R.M. 2847 (9th Cir. 1978) and University of Chicago v. NLRB, 514 F. 2d 942, 89 L.R.R.M. 2113 (7th Cir. 1975).

9. 268 N.L.R.B. at 602, 115 L.R.R.M. at 1067.

10. Id. at 603, 115 L.R.R.M. at 1068.

11. Discussed, ante, at section 3 of Chapter IV. There and in Chapter VI (note 9 and accompanying text) we make the same point that the Board is about to make here.

12. 268 N.L.R.B. at 603, 115 L.R.R.M. at 1067.

13. 268 N.L.R.B. at 605, 115 L.R.R.M. at 1069.

14. Automobile Workers v. NLRB, 765 F. 2d at 175 (D.C. Cir. 1985).

15. 765 F. 2d at 184.

16. Otis Elevator Co., 269 N.L.R.B. 891, 115 L.R.R.M. 1281 (1984).

17. 255 N.L.R.B. at 235, 106 L.R.R.M. at 1343 (1981).

18. 269 N.L.R.B. at 891, 115 L.R.R.M. at 1281. The Board added (ibid.) that its understanding of the construction of section 8(d) by the Court in First National Maintenance is "best explicated" by the following excerpt from the opinion of Justice Stewart: "If as I think clear, the purpose of section 8(d) is to describe a limited area subject to the duty of collective bargaining, those management decisions which are fundamental to the basic direction of a corporate enterprise or which impinge only indirectly upon employment security should be excluded from the area." 379 U.S. at 223.

19. Id. at 892, 115 L.R.R.M. at 1282.

20. Ibid., 452 U.S. at 678-79.

21. Ibid. Here and elsewhere it is clear that (unlike the "old" Board and Mr. Lubbers, who saw union labor costs as immune and inescapable) this Board sees them as equating with what the Court in First National Maintenance (citing Justice Stewart) called the "employment relationship," that is to say, they involve matter which is within the ambit of compulsory decision bargaining, but only to the point of impasse. This distinction is important in understanding the new directions charted by the Reagan Board. It mentions "labor costs" as an important factor almost as often as the "old" Board did but, as we have just seen, the meaning, in terms of the union agreement and the duty to bargain, is quite different.

22. 269 N.L.R.B. at 892, 115 L.R.R.M. at 1282-83. Emphasis in original.

23. 269 N.L.R.B. at 893, 115 L.R.R.M. at 1283.

24. Ibid. Emphasis added.

25. Ibid. The Board here cites a case in which a federal appellate court held that there was no duty to bargain over a decision to merge. Such decisions, said the court, require a secrecy, flexibility, and quickness "antithetical to collective bargaining." Machinists v. Northeast Airlines, 473 F. 2d 549, 557, 80 L.R.R.M. 2197, 2203 (1st Cir. 1972).

26. The Board soon had occasion to apply this dictum in an actual case (Gar Wood-Detroit Truck Equipment, Inc., discussed next) and it held that the contracting arrangement in that case was not subject to mandatory decision bargaining.

27. 269 N.L.R.B. at 893, 115 L.R.R.M. at 1283. It is important to bear in mind throughout this discussion that, in contrast to the former Board, what this Board means when it says that such decisions are "within section 8(d)" is that they are subject to mandatory bargaining—but only to impasse. They are not, as the Carter Board had it, decisions that it is impermissible to carry out in the absence of union consent.

28. 269 N.L.R.B. at 894, 115 L.R.R.M. at 1283-84. Presumably, this is because the decision in *Milwaukee Spring* "turned on" labor costs. This gratuitous remark is interesting, nonetheless, because the Board shied away from this issue in the course of its opinion in *Milwaukee Spring II*. (*See* 268 N.L.R.B. at 601 n. 5, 115 L.R.R.M. at 1066 n. 5.)

29. 269 N.L.R.B. at 894, 115 L.R.R.M. at 1284.

30. *Ibid.* So far as we have been able to ascertain, there have been no further proceedings in *Otis*.

31. We shall, however, find it necessary, from time to time, to advert to Member Dennis's analysis, in order to make clear our discussion of the conclusions which she draws from it. Accordingly, it will be useful to have in mind the three categories into which, as she reads it, *FNM* divided management decisions and which she summarizes (269 N.L.R.B. at 895-96, 115 L.R.R.M. at 1286) as follows:

> Category I [all quotations are from Justice Blackmun's opinion] "decisions, such as choice of advertising and promotion, product type and design, and financing arrangements, have only an indirect and attenuated impact on the employment relationship." Category II "decisions, such as the order of succession of layoffs and recalls, production quotas, and work rules, are almost exclusively" an aspect of the employment relationship. Category III decisions have "a direct impact on employment," but have as their "focus" only the economic profitability of the employer's operation, a concern wholly apart from the employment relationship. 452 U.S. at 676-77.

32. 269 N.L.R.B. at 897, 115 L.R.R.M. at 1287-88.

33. 269 N.L.R.B. at 897 n. 8, 115 L.R.R.M. at 1288 n. 8. We call attention to Member Dennis's statement that no bargaining is required in "partial closing" situations. As we read it, this amounts to an interpretation that no decision bargaining will *ever* be required in those "Category III" situations which involve a partial closing in response to economic necessity, and we ourselves viewed Justice Blackmun's burden-benefits formula as leading, almost inevitably, to that conclusion—at least in cases like the one before him. Member Dennis appears to go further and to hold that although there *may* be "Category III " cases in which decision bargaining will be required, a partial closing is not one of them. Neither, for more obvious reasons, is a sale. A plant relocation, on the other hand, may very well be subject to decision bargaining in the Dennis analysis.

34. 269 N.L.R.B. at 899, 115 L.R.R.M. at 1290. Member Dennis appears to be testing for "amenability" to collective bargaining. But *see* the main opinion (at note 22, *supra*), stating the criterion to be "the essence of the decision itself," rather than "a union's ability to offer alternatives."

35. *Ibid.*

36. *Ibid.*, 452 U.S. at 679.

37. *Id.* at 900, 115 L.R.R.M. at 1290.

38. *Id.* at 898, 115 L.R.R.M. at 1288-89. The cases discussed include several which we also discussed in our treatment of the period between *Fibreboard* and *First National Maintenance.*

39. 269 N.L.R.B. at 898-99, 115 L.R.R.M. at 1289.

40. 269 N.L.R.B. at 900, 115 L.R.R.M. at 1285.

41. In that respect, the *Otis* majority was in harmony with Justice Blackmun, who had said (452 U.S. at 681, 107 L.R.R.M. at 2711): "There is no dispute that the union must be given a significant opportunity to bargain about these matters of job security as part of the 'effects' bargaining mandated by Section 8(a)(5)."

And he added: "And, under Section 8(a)(5), bargaining over the effects of a decision must be conducted in a meaningful manner and at a meaningful time, and the Board may impose sanctions to insure its adequacy." But *see, ante,* Chapter IV, note 36.

42. In footnote 15 to the Court's opinion, Justice Blackmun says (452 U.S. at 677):

> There is no doubt that petitioner was under a duty to bargain about the results or effects of its decision to stop the work at Greenpark, or that it violated that duty. Petitioner consented to the enforcement of the Board's order concerning bargaining over the effects of the closing and has reached agreement with the union on severance pay.

43. Effects bargaining, it is worth remarking, not only does not (or will not usually) impede the decision-making process the way decision bargaining does, but also it raises no questions of "amenability," since it is dealing with the stuff of ordinary collective bargaining (e.g., severance pay, application of seniority, transfer rights).

44. 274 N.L.R.B. at 113, 118 L.R.R.M. at 1417 (1985).

45. *Id.* at 113-114, 118 L.R.R.M. at 1418.

46. The decision of the ALJ, from which some of the foregoing facts are derived, is attached to 274 N.L.R.B. at 113, but is not reprinted in L.R.R.M.

47. The remedy is of interest. In order to keep the effects bargaining from being a sterile ritual taking place in the face of a *fait accompli* as far as the contracting out was concerned, the Board used what it called "limited backpay" [sic] to build some leverage for the union into the bargaining situation. The back pay would start soon after the date of the Board's order and continue until the occurrence of one or another of several possible eventualities (e.g., agreement, impasse, etc.). No one would receive less than two weeks' pay, under the terms of the Board's remedy.

48. 274 N.L.R.B. at 117, 118 L.R.R.M. at 1420.

49. In part this may be due to the fact that the Act deals only with unionized employees, who comprise somewhat less than 20 percent of the work force. In the next chapter we deal with job rights as they exist, or may come into being, other than by way of the National Labor Relations Act.

Chapter VIII

1. We now substitute "job rights" for "workers' rights" for the purpose of suggesting the broader scope of our inquiry in this chapter. To some extent, the two terms have been used interchangeably in the debate over rights-in-the-job, although the *content* of either term tends to depend on the speaker. However, in view of the fact that we used "workers' rights" so consistently in describing the rights of *unionized* employees, we feel that a switch

in terminology at this point is desirable to denote the fact that we will be dealing now with a broader class of employees (including managerial and other nonunionized employees), and our survey contemplates a broader range of job-related issues, some of which will not necessarily involve the closing or relocation of a plant—our primary focus up to now.

2. To the extent that the "property rights" terminology is not purely polemical in purpose, it probably stems from a combination of compassion and misunderstanding of how our system works. What job rights advocates are seeking is a compassionate solution to a human problem. The problem, in their view, is that the economic vicissitudes of the employer, which cause the elimination of the job, thereby fall unfairly on the employee. Job rights advocates do not feel that the employee should be without recourse in those unfortunate circumstances. Yet, the logic of our system of law requires that a *remedy* must be founded upon a *right* whose protection or enforcement or vindication the remedy exists to accomplish. Hence, by a process not unlike the creation of a word by what lexicographers know as backward formation, we find a right being asserted to exist in order to establish a foundation for a remedy. It is probably something like this that proponents of so-called "economic democracy" have in mind when, pressing for systemic political change, they argue for a right of "participation" by workers in managerial decisions which affect them. Among other things, this has led to an argument, in effect, for decision bargaining to be extended to *all* employees, not just those covered by the National Labor Relations Act. This notion, along with the rest of the case for worker participation in management decision making, is handled with his customary thoroughness by Professor Richard J. McKenzie in his essay entitled *Justice as Participation: Should Workers Be Given Management Rights?* Center for the Study of American Business (Washington University, St. Louis), Formal Pamphlet No. 71 (1985).

3. *See,* generally, O'Connell, "The Labor Arbitrator: Judge or Legislator?" in *Proceedings of the Eighteenth Annual Meeting of the National Academy of Arbitrators* (Washington: The Bureau of National Affairs, 1965).

4. C. Bakaly, Jr. and J. Grossman, *Modern Law of Employment Contracts* (New York: Law & Business, Inc./Harcourt Brace Jovanovich, 1983) at 1 (hereafter cited as *Bakaly & Grossman*).

5. R. McKenzie, *Competing Visions* (Washington: Cato Institute, 1985) at 131.

6. In order to sharpen our focus on the common-law employment-at-will doctrine, we shall ignore in the discussion which follows the abridgement of that doctrine by the National Labor Relations Act, beginning in 1935, and its modification by union contract provisions requiring "just cause" for discharge.

7. *See* Mich. Comp. Laws ann. sec. 15.361-15.369 (West 1981). But *see* Bakaly & Grossman, Chapter 9 at 120-22.

8. Peterman v. International Brotherhood of Teamsters, 174 Cal. App. 2d 184, 29 Cal. Rptr. 399, 344 P. 2d 25 (1959).

9. Touissant v. Blue Cross & Blue Shield of Michigan, 408 Mich. 479, 292 NW 2d 880 (1980).

10. Kirk LaShelle Co. v. Paul Armstrong Co., 263 NY 79, 87, 188 NE 163, 167 (1933).

11. *See* Bakaly & Grossman, Ch. 9 at 130-32 and cases cited.

12. Carson v. Atari Inc., California Superior Court, County of Santa Clara, No. 530743.

13. *Id.*, Third Amended Complaint, ¶10.

14. One major defense presented in the pretrial stage was the claim that the California courts do not have jurisdiction, because the National Labor Relations Act applies. It appears that there was a union organizing campaign prior to the shutdown, and the

defendants claimed that the alleged job assurances were all given in connection with that campaign, making the case an NLRB matter.

15. Defendants' "Memorandum of Points and Authorities in Support of Demurrers and Motions to Strike," 58-59.

16. *See, passim,* Bakaly & Grossman, Chapters 1, 9, 10.

17. Chapter V, *ante,* at 56. It is true that Justice Blackmun's *dictum* was uttered in the context of management's mandatory duty to provide a union with notice and an opportunity to bargain over the management decision—issues not involved in the *Atari* class action. Nevertheless, it is not without significance that the Supreme Court has already indicated some tendency to sympathize with this sort of management problem.

18. The complaint alleges a violation of the California Labor Code, section 2922, which provides that an employment having no specified term may be terminated "at the will of either party on notice to the other." The parties disagree as to the obligation (if any) which this section imposed on *Atari.* The plaintiffs clearly hope to have the court invest section 2922 with a real and measurable obligation of notice.

Chapter IX

1. If we may be pardoned for a descent to the nuts-and-bolts level of negotiations, this means that unions might seek a promise that jobs will not be eliminated during the life of the contract, but, in that case, they must be prepared (as they generally have not been in the past) to buy this large concession with a modified wage package. They will find, in all likelihood, that such a concession evokes a great deal of amenability toward "closing rights" on the part of the employer—and, indeed, the savings that might be achieved in payroll costs pursuant to such a concession might well provide an employer with a kitty out of which the expenses of severance pay, retraining, and other plant closing costs might be met.